MICROECONOMIC PRINCIPLES IN ACTION

MICROECONOMIC PRINCIPLES IN ACTION

■ **Robert L. Moore**
Occidental College

■ **James D. Whitney**
Occidental College

 PRENTICE HALL, Englewood Cliffs, New Jersey 07632

Library of Congress Cataloging-in-Publication Data

Microeconomic principles in action / [edited by] Robert L. Moore and
    James D. Whitney.
        p.   cm.
    ISBN 0-13-582420-6
    1. Microeconomics.   I. Moore, Robert L.   II. Whitney,
James D.
HB172.M587   1990   89–39462
338.5—dc20   CIP

Editorial/production supervision and
    interior design: **Esther S. Koehn**
Cover design: **Ben Santora**
Manufacturing buyer: **Laura Crossland**

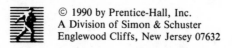 © 1990 by Prentice-Hall, Inc.
A Division of Simon & Schuster
Englewood Cliffs, New Jersey 07632

Printed in the United States of America
10 9 8 7 6 5 4 3 2 1

ISBN 0-13-582420-6

Prentice-Hall International (UK) Limited, *London*
Prentice-Hall of Australia Pty. Limited, *Sydney*
Prentice-Hall Canada Inc., *Toronto*
Prentice-Hall Hispanoamericana, S.A., *Mexico City*
Prentice-Hall of India Private Limited, *New Delhi*
Prentice-Hall of Japan, Inc., *Tokyo*
Simon & Schuster Asia Pte. Ltd., *Singapore*
Editora Prentice-Hall do Brasil, Ltda., *Rio de Janeiro*

Contents

Preface   *xiii*

PART I *Introduction: Scarcity, Opportunity Cost, and Markets*   **1**

1   A Divorced Spouse's Professional Degree:
    Is It Community Property?   *1*
        Los Angeles Times

2   MBA Students Learn the Cost of Education   *5*
        Wall Street Journal

3   Price of Babies Rising in Wider Black Market   *8*
        New York Times

4   Back to the Draft: It's More Economical,
    and It's Right   *10*
        Los Angeles Times

PART II *Market Fundamentals: Supply and Demand*   **12**

5   Europe's Drivers Don't Reduce Gasoline Use
    Despite Soaring Prices   *12*
        Wall Street Journal

6   The Price of Beer Rises at a Heady Pace,
    but Americans Are Thirstier Than Ever   *15*
        Wall Street Journal

7   Wheeling for Wages   *17*
     Los Angeles Times

8   Mink Farming Is Growing More Scarce
     as Costs Rise and Fur Demand Declines   *19*
     Wall Street Journal

9   Moonshiners in South Find Sales
     Are Down as Their Costs Go Up   *21*
     Wall Street Journal

10   Consumers and Coffee   *24*
     Wall Street Journal

11   U.S. Faces Oversupply of Doctors by 2000   *25*
     Milwaukee Journal

12   Santa Monica—Only the Elite Need Apply   *27*
     Los Angeles Times

13   The Real Costs of a Higher Minimum Wage   *32*
     Business Week

14   Push to Snuff Out Subsidy Lights Fears   *35*
     Los Angeles Times

PART III   *Demand in More Detail*   **38**

15   British Officials Aren't About to Fine
     Ticket Scalpers for Making Huge Profit   *38*
     Los Angeles Times

16   Price Hike: Coming Soon to a Theatre Near You?   *39*
     Los Angeles Times

17   Despite Fare Rise, Taxi Fleets
     Report New Losses Again   *41*
     New York Times

18 X-FLIX TAX   *42*
       Wall Street Journal

PART IV   *Competitive Supply*   **43**

19 Major League Averages   *43*

20 1987 Tax Rate Schedules   *45*

21 Hertz Corp. Study   *47*
       Los Angeles Times

22 Airline Takes the Marginal Route   *48*
       Business Week

23 On Average and Marginal Cost   *51*
       Wall Street Journal

24 More May Be Too Much   *52*
       Los Angeles Times

25 Lag in Tanker Business Puts the Squeeze
on Builders and Owners—as Well as Banks   *55*
       Wall Street Journal

PART V   *Supply with Imperfect Competition*   **57**

26 A Supremely Unsettling Smorgasbord   *57*
       Sports Illustrated

27 The Market for Principles
of Economics Texts   *59*
       The Margin

28 Trade-A-Beta   *63*

29 American Air Accused of Bid to Fix Prices   *65*
       Wall Street Journal

30 Market Forces and Discord Stymie Cartels   67
     Wall Street Journal

31 23 Colleges in East Adjust Aid
to Avert Bidding for Students   69
     New York Times

32 Timing of Changes in Prices of 99%
Plus Primary Aluminum Ingot   71

33 Copy Cat Service Tells
"Other Side" of Pricing Battle   72
     Harvard Crimson

34 The Drive Is on to Deregulate Taxis   73
     Business Week

35 Mr. Miller of the FTC Takes on the Doctors   75
     Wall Street Journal

36 Beer Wholesalers Push for Monopoly   78
     Los Angeles Times

PART VI   *Resource Markets*   **81**

37 Fernando Hits Jackpot for Million   81
     Los Angeles Times

38 Nursing Shortage: Hospitals Feel
Effects of Feminism, Low Salaries   83
     Cape Cod Times

39 Fast-Food Chains Act to Offset
the Effects of Minimum-Pay Rise   85
     Wall Street Journal

40 Housing Dispute Spurs Michigan Farmers
to Switch to Machines from Migrant Help   88
     Wall Street Journal

41   When a College Signs a Franchise,
     Benefits Can Spill Out Everywhere   91
          Wall Street Journal

42   1.9% APR: At This Rate, It's So Easy
     to Drive a New Chevy Home   93

43   State's Lottery "Millionaires"
     Will Be Somewhat Less Than   95
          Los Angeles Times

44   Carter Sees Solar Heater
     as Example and Symbol   97
          Boston Globe

45   Benefit of B.A. Is Greater Than Ever   98
          Wall Street Journal

PART VII   Market Successes and Failures   **101**

46   Why Calls Should Cost a Quarter   101
          New York Times

47   Braude's Ban on New Billboards
     Falls One Vote Short   102
          Los Angeles Times

48   The Cuts in Federal Aid   104
          Newsweek

49   What Cost a Life? EPA Asks Tacoma   108
          Los Angeles Times

50   How to Break Up Traffic Jams   112
          Wall Street Journal

51 Can Software Be Made Safe from Piracy?   *115*

   Los Angeles Times

52 Economic Policy Can Be
Hard-Headed—and Soft-Hearted   *118*

   Business Week

Preface

This book consists of a collection of newspaper articles and related items that should help beginning students apply some key microeconomic principles. Most of the selections have already been used as exercises by our own students at Occidental College and Harvard University. Students have consistently rated the working of the exercises that accompany these articles as one of the most useful instructional devices for learning the basic principles of microeconomics.

The major purpose of the book is to help students enjoy the study of economics while they gain a better understanding of its basic principles. Evidence strongly indicates that students in introductory microeconomics courses retain little of what they learn unless they become interested enough to make use of their knowledge outside the classroom. And learning how to use and apply the principles of the classroom is no easy feat. It takes lots of practice. We hope that this book will enable students to learn how to apply what they have learned and provide them with the incentive to do so.

Microeconomic Principles in Action is meant to accompany any of the major "Principles of Economics" textbooks used in courses that emphasize microeconomics. However, it is important to realize that the book is neither a "readings" book nor a "workbook/study guide." It differs from the latter in that all the problems here are based on actual applications of the material appearing in the selections. Often, the author of a selection has made a key analytical error that a student with a knowledge of economics can identify. The book differs from conventional readings books in that it emphasizes very short applications of principles that directly relate to key microeconomic concepts. The selections are chosen so as to induce the student to apply only a small number of principles at a time. We believe that student appreciation of these principles at work in their daily lives generates a more lasting interest in economics than is possible from exposure only to polished discussions of "current policy issues."

HOW TO USE THE BOOK

To the Student: Since this book is not like a textbook, it requires a different approach. Before reading a selection, review the brief description of the selection and the type of questions that you will be asked about it. Then review the questions that accompany the selection. After you have read the selection, write out complete answers to the questions. This is important because the writing will help you think about and retain what you are learning.

To the Instructor: The Instructor's Manual will provide you with detailed solutions to all the questions as well as a fuller description of the selection than the one that appears in the book. You will find advice that will help you decide whether a particular article is appropriate for your specific course. The organization is fairly straightforward and along the lines of almost all the major principles text. Even if your course structure varies somewhat from the format of our book, we feel this should not cause any major problems. We welcome any comments you might have about the articles and their usefulness to your students.

ACKNOWLEDGMENTS

Our greatest debt in putting this book together goes to our former introductory economics students, both at Occidental College and at Harvard University, who have read these selections and attempted to answer the questions. They have contributed greatly to the quality of the questions. In a few instances others were responsible for bringing a particular article to our attention, and we would especially like to thank Eleanor Brown (Pomona College), Jeff Wolcowitz (Harvard University), and Elisabeth Allison (formerly of Harvard University). We cannot recall how some of the selections first came to our attention and sincerely regret any omissions in this regard. We would also like to thank our colleagues at Occidental College for helping us stay excited about teaching introductory economics. Since one of our goals is to help students learn through discovering the errors made by others, we claim responsibility for any remaining errors on our part and hope that students learn from them as well.

Robert L. Moore
James D. Whitney

MICROECONOMIC PRINCIPLES IN ACTION

The opportunity cost of education and training plays a controversial role in this article about divorce. The wife, Janet Sullivan, filed for a divorce after working for ten years while her husband, Mark, completed a degree, internship, and residency in urology. As part of the divorce settlement, Janet decided to seek compensation for her investment in Mark's medical training. The article focuses on the economic costs and benefits of education, and it illustrates both positive and normative issues in economics.

A Divorced Spouse's Professional Degree: Is It Community Property?

By ROXANE ARNOLD

After 10 years working as an accountant while husband Mark completed medical school, an internship and residency in urology, Janet Sullivan decided their marriage was over. She walked out, taking their young daughter with her.

When the couple filed for divorce two years later in Santa Ana, there wasn't much to divide in the way of community property—some used furniture and two cars that weren't paid for.

Janet decided to try for more—a share of Mark's earnings as a doctor.

On Tuesday, the California Supreme Court is scheduled to take up the Sullivan case, which centers on Janet's claim that she should be compensated for putting her ex-husband through medical school. It is a contention that has jolted medical and professional groups and unleashed a storm of clashing views.

The case has become a *cause celebre* among those who see it as the "most important women's issue of the day" and has prompted at least one California assemblyman to draft so-called Sullivan legislation to take care of former spouses like Janet.

It also has spurred Mark's fellow doctors in Orange County to establish a legal defense fund to battle what they call a "threat to all people who have a degree" and has convinced the powerful California Medical Assn. to enter the fray on behalf of its members.

"The ramifications of the case are shocking for some," said UCLA law professor Grace Blumberg. "It means that people could be paying through their noses for the rest of their professional lives."

Although a rash of cases involving professional degrees have been heard in courtrooms across the country in the last two years, few have been heard in state high courts and none is likely to have the national impact of a Sullivan decision, since the California Supreme Court is regarded as a trend-setter in family law.

Unlike most other states, where judges have discretion in dividing marital assets, California is bound by a no-fault divorce law that requires an even distribution of property accumulated during a marriage regardless of who wanted to end the marriage. The state definition of community property includes furniture, real estate and other tangible assets as well as intangibles such as pensions and professional reputations that have recognized value.

"California doesn't have the flexibility of other states," said Blumberg, the co-author of a friend-of-the-court brief on Janet's behalf. "The California Supreme Court is not going to be able to fudge the issue.

"In other states, courts can give her something without giving her too much. In California, it has got to be an all-or-nothing proposition. The future earnings represented by her husband's degree is either property or it isn't, and she gets half or she gets nothing."

The court actually faces two decisions. Justices must first determine whether Mark's medical degree is community property and if so, how to measure its future value.

1

Ultimately, however, the court's decision will affect not only physicians but those who earn professional degrees while married.

Some argue that a degree-is-property ruling could apply to every faltering marriage, creating nightmares for the courts and never-ending entanglements for couples who just want to split. Others predict it will produce a booming market for pre-nuptial agreements and bring romance to an end.

"It's not going to be very good for the couples," said Sacramento attorney Fred J. Hiestand, who filed a brief for the California Medical Assn. Hiestand said that the association decided to become involved in the case when its members agreed "they didn't want their degrees to become a target for a vindictive spouse or a potential future creditor."

Hiestand said that "when you start considering a degree property, you open a potential floodgate. . . . I don't see how you can distinguish between a medical degree and any other kind of degree—a college degree, a junior college degree. There is going to be a burgeoning business in evaluating degrees . . . it will take a lot more time to unwind a marriage."

When the Sullivans were divorced, there was no indication that theirs would become a landmark case. As Janet's attorney, Patricia Herzog, explains it, there was just a nagging feeling that something wasn't fair.

The judge who handled the Sullivan divorce trial decided not to consider the medical degree in the divorce settlement, based on then-existent case law. Janet, who earns enough to support herself, was not eligible for alimony. She was, however, awarded $250 a month in child support payments even though the couple was awarded joint custody of their child.

In January, 1981, the 4th District Court of Appeal took Janet's side and sent the case back to the trial court to determine what was due to her.

Eight months later, the appellate court reversed itself, finding that professional training is not part of the marital kitty because it does not fit traditional concepts of property. The justices who changed their minds said that the unusual reversal resulted from a closer review of the case.

By the time the California Supreme Court agreed to hear the Sullivan case, more than a dozen other states were grappling with the same issue and a handful of high courts had rendered opinions. Most of the cases involved medical and legal degrees. In one state, though, it was a master's in business administration; in another, a doctorate of philosophy. Apparently the degree holders in these cases have been men.

Although few courts have ruled that a degree is property, most have tried to give the woman some reimbursement for her time and trouble. But the disparity in the judgments has resulted mostly in confusion.

Very Confusing

"Everyone is doing their own thing trying to fit in with traditional definitions of property . . . to try to achieve equity in one way or another," said New York divorce layer Doris Freed. "It's very confusing and it's wrong . . . you can get so hung up on terminology that you come up with zilch."

Two cases heard in New York last summer illustrate the chaos. One trial court judge, calling a husband's medical license the only valuable asset of the nine-year marriage, awarded the schoolteacher wife almost $190,000. Weeks later, an appellate court considering another case held that a medical license was not property and gave the wife nothing.

The record is just as muddled in other states. In Minnesota, one wife received $11,400 after a court determined she was due reimbursement for the amount she contributed to her husband's education. In a similar case in Kentucky, the spouse was awarded $11,600. In Illinois and Arizona, two wives came away empty-handed. In Oklahoma, a doctor's wife was awarded an extra $39,000 in alimony based on the husband's increased earning ability.

A few states have tried to legislate consistency. Lawmakers in Wisconsin added a statute providing for some compensation for spouses who have contributed to their mates' education. In Indiana, legislators enacted a provision calling for reimbursement of tuition, books or other fees if there is little else to divide.

If the California Supreme Court decides to classify degrees as property, some legal experts believe there would be a great impact on other states.

"It would be such an extreme, unusual step," said University of Missouri law professor Joan Krauskopf. "It would be highly significant because it would be the first Supreme Court in the country to classify a degree as property. It would highlight for the whole country how important this issue is."

Krauskopf acknowledged that the ramifications of legally recognizing one spouse's role in the education of the other are staggering, but she said it is "one of the most important women's issues in the country."

"It is still the woman who is putting the man through professional school, the woman who doesn't develop her own earning capacity . . . the MDs around the country are scared to death they might have to give some reimbursement to that woman who put them through medical school, who suffered through an internship with them—the woman they then walked out on."

"The whole principle of community property in California is that all assets, all property belongs to both," said Stanford sociologist Lenore Weitzman. "Our courts are making a mockery of that . . . by letting the husband hide his gold behind his back. The educational degree is the jewelry in the marriage."

UCLA's Blumberg said that calling a degree property is the logical next step for a Supreme Court that already has classified intangibles such as pensions and professional reputation or goodwill as marital assets.

"The notion of a professional education kind of piggybacks on these earlier rulings," Blumberg said. "A professional degree is just another intangible, something you can't package, but it is still property."

To those who would argue that the value of a professional degree defies calculation, Blumberg answered, "it is a little complicated, but it is doable."

But California Medical Assn. attorney Hiestand predicts evaluating degrees will "open a real Pandora's box. It will be a fight of the experts, a great boon to economists . . . and a step backward."

Southwestern University law professor Max Goodman predicted that a court-ordered payoff to Janet will mean "you won't be able to settle any case . . . in every marriage, there is enhanced earning of some sort, either by way of education or more experience or promotions. If Mrs. Sullivan's theory is accepted by the court, you're going to have these problems of enhanced earning ability in every single dissolution case."

Economists and lawyers already have been working to come up with ways to value degrees and divide the earnings.

[A] One formula projects what an average degree holder would earn over a lifetime with the degree and subtracts projected earnings without it. The difference is reduced through a series of equations to its value in current dollars. A former spouse would get half that amount through installments with interest.

A second formula depends on the professional's actual work. The supporting spouse would be entitled to half of what is earned during a time span comparable to the period it took to earn the degree.

To make such formulas work, Blumberg says, the degree must be worth something. What sets professional degrees apart from job promotions earned during marriage or courses taken for fun is what she called the "opportunity cost."

"For Dr. Sullivan, the real cost of his education was not books, it was not tuition; it was being absent from the labor force for 10 years doing whatever he

could have done as a bachelor of science," Blumberg said. "These people would have had lots of money if one of the spouses hadn't undertaken 10 years of self-enhancement."

Attorney Goodman, who will help argue Mark Sullivan's case before the Supreme Court, admits it is that kind of "perceived injustice" that has him worried as the court date nears.

"It's the gut-level reaction," Goodman said. "He walks out instant doctor and she walks out with a baby . . . and so she should get paid somehow." In the Sullivans' case, Mark is now a urologist in Laguna Hills and Janet is a medical accountant and living in a rented house in Laguna Beach.

Marriage Is Risk

Goodman argues that marriage is a risk under any circumstances. To deal with it otherwise would be unjust to Dr. Sullivan.

"Implicit in her (Janet's) theory is there is an obligation to work while you are married, and if you don't work, you can be sued for damages," he said. "That's not true . . . there is the expectation that the marriage will last. But if it doesn't, that is the risk she took. That's the way the cookie crumbled, that's the way the marriage crumbled . . . there is no injustice in this."

The California Legislature already has reached that same conclusion, Goodman said.

Lawmakers recently amended community property laws by making educational debts an exception to the 50-50 distribution rule. The spouse receiving the education must pay its costs as part of a divorce settlement.

"The Legislature could have said that education is an asset, but they didn't," Goodman said. "The courts should respect that."

Not all legislators agree.

Assemblyman Alister McAlister (D-Milpitas) is drafting a measure that includes earning capacity in community property.

[B] "The most important property that most couples have when they separate is the earning capacity of the husband," McAlister said. "The wife should not be left high and dry . . . there is a need to protect her."

What sociologist Weitzman calls a "blueprint for marriage"—the pre-nuptial agreement—also would protect warring spouses.

Although many believe signing contracts does not make for a good marriage, others say the pacts simplify the ending of a relationship. Whether pre-nuptial agreements will be used widely is another question.

"Marriage contracts are one way of handling

things, but they're not used that often and I don't think that's likely to change," attorney Herzog said. "People marry when their eyes are filled with stars and their hearts with love. They don't consider divorce."

Blumberg countered that a Supreme Court ruling that puts professional degrees up for grabs could change that.

"I suppose if people keep doing this," Blumberg predicted, "there will come a time when your indoctrination packet going into medical school will have information on how to write contracts. It will be there along with your Blue Cross card." ∎

QUESTIONS

1. Suppose the court decided to award Janet a "refund" equal to half the investment the couple had made in Mark's medical training. What items should be included in determining the amount of this refund? In other words, what items make up the economic (opportunity) cost of Mark's medical training?

2. If you had been the judge hearing the Janet Sullivan case, what would you have awarded Janet? Briefly support your decision.

3. Passage A of the article covers two options for measuring the value of a degree:
    a. How do the two options differ?
    b. Which option more accurately measures the expected return on an investment in education (including your own)?

4. For each of the two sentences in passage B of the article, decide whether the sentence constitutes a positive or a normative statement, and briefly explain your decision in each case.

Informational note: The judge in this case awarded Janet Sullivan half of Mark's earnings for the first ten years of his medical practice. After the case, the state of California passed the "Sullivan Law," which specified that awards for education investments should not exceed total expenditures on tuition and books.

This article considers some of the many ways to "ration" scarce goods, and it illustrates the difference between market and nonmarket mechanisms for allocating these goods. The article describes the "market mechanism" set up at the Graduate School of Business at the University of Chicago for class registration, rationing of computer time, and interviews with potential employers.

MBA Students Learn the Cost of Education

By JOHN CURLEY

Summer-session students registering at the University of Chicago business school today won't have to line up at dawn or take their chances in a lottery to get the classes they want. They'll *buy* their courses.

Chicago's business school has been teaching a free-market philosophy for years, starting long before Milton Friedman, a former professor at the school, made such an approach the stuff of a best-selling book and a Nobel prize. Now the school is bringing its teaching out of the classroom.

Starting today, students are bidding for the courses they want with points handed out by the dean's office. How much will it take to get into a popular professor's class? "The market will decide the price," says Stephen T. Schreiber, associate dean of students.

Classes won't be the only commodities getting the capitalist treatment. Students will also bid for computer time and interviews with potential employers.

Campus Trend

The innovation is typical of those that many business schools are trying in response to student pressure for fairer means of allocation. Stanford business school has heeded students' request for a ranking system that tries to match each student with seven companies he or she wants to talk to. Northwestern's school of management, meanwhile, has melded the Chicago and Stanford systems: It gives students 100 points every two weeks to bid for interviews, plus five "priority points" that all but assure a student at least a few important interviews.

Chicago doesn't believe in that kind of safety net. It prefers a free-market system that "really forces stu-

Going Rate For Courses		
Point Cost*	Professor	Course
11,000	Merton H. Miller	Corporate Finance
8,000	James H. Lorie	Topics in Investment
4,000	Edward T. Lazear	Microeconomics
2,000	Hillel J. Einhorn	Cognitive Models of Judgment
1,500	Robert Blattberg	Marketing
1,000	Jonathan E. Ingersoll	Investment
*Prices as of last fall.		

dents to choose their priorities and allocate their resources," as Mr. Schreiber puts it.

[A] At registration, students get 8,000 points plus 1,000 for each course they have completed. Then they submit four possible course schedules, telling how much they're bidding for each. If a class will hold, say, 100 students, the 100 highest bidders will get in. However, in a slight softening of the harsh rules in the real world, students won't be charged as much as they bid but only as much as the 100th-place bidder offered.

The system was tried out last March in the school's night program in downtown Chicago. Of the 1,000 students involved, only 34 didn't get any of their choices. The school says that was a marked improvement from the old system, under which students who had completed the most courses got to sign up first, but had to go in alphabetical order.

Free to Choose

"I really think it's the way to do things," says Michael Von derPorten, a first-year student. "It gives you more control over your life."

It also provides the faculty a handy way to practice what it preaches. Richard J. Thain, dean for career development and counseling, says that "all of us have been so tickled, because it's such a good example of putting the market philosophy to work." Besides, it helps him know which companies interest students most. And other faculty members say the bidding makes it easier to allocate classroom space.

There still are problems to be ironed out. New students may be confused and unable to estimate the market price for classes or job interviews. That happened at the nightschool trial run, when some students bid only 50 points for courses that were selling for 200 or 300 points. (The highest bid, by the way, was 40,000 points for Merton Miller's corporation-finance class; but 11,000 was enough to win a place.)

Dean Schreiber concedes the problems. "Students don't understand all the details, which is logical, since *we* don't understand all the details," he says. The administration is thinking about scheduling classes on how to bid for classes.

[B] Problems also have arisen in the computer-time auction. Students get 100 "computer dollars" at enrollment, plus added currency for every course they've completed. But some students find their appetite for electronic aid breaks their budget. The result is a black market in computer cash, in which the going rate is one computer dollar for half a real one. It's estimated that about 5% of the future executives at the University of Chicago trade in the black market.

To bid for job interviews, students are given a basic ration of 350 points. They get an added 221 points each fall and 371 more in the spring, when more companies come to campus. Two weeks before an interview, students punch their bids into a computer.

Dean Thain says recruiters like the system because it assures them that the people they're talking to are truly interested. It also helps them know how they're doing; noticing unusually low bids for a large industrial company two years ago, Mr. Thain advised its recruiters to change the job description from "foreman" to "production assistant," increase the salary and raise the concern's campus profile through beer parties and talks by executives. The next year the company hired three Chicago MBAs.

The University of Chicago's venture into the free market comes only after the system has proved itself in other areas of student life. Every year, students bid for a food concession and then borrow money from the school to run it, commonly making a nice profit. And this year students sold stock to finance the annual spring follies. They returned $26 for every $10 invested in a show entitled "Capitalist Pyg-Malion." ∎

QUESTIONS

1. Which classes, if any, at your college or university are "economic" ("scarce") goods?
2. What mechanisms are used at your school to determine who gets into such classes—e.g., waiting in line, college major, etc.?
3. Much of microeconomics is really about the advantages and disadvantages of using the "market mechanism" to allocate scarce goods. Can you think of any advantages/disadvantages of using the "market mechanism" described in this article compared with the procedure used at your school? Explain.
4. Milton Friedman, in his book *Free to Choose*, claims that one of the functions that "market prices" perform in a free market is the transmission of information. How do the prices that result from the "market mechanism" at the University of Chicago perform this function? (Provide specific examples from the article.)
5. Consider passage A:
   a. What do you think is the purpose of the formula determining the number of points a student will get to "spend"?
   b. How does this feature of the University of Chicago "market" differ from the market for, say, apples or gasoline or expensive housing?
   c. Do the "harsh rules in the real world" really require you to pay as much as you would be willing to bid for a particular good? Explain. *Hint:* Consider the maximum amount you would be willing to pay for one of your favorite books. Is your answer identical to the actual market price?
6. Consider passage B: Economists (and economic textbooks) claim that "voluntary exchange" is beneficial to both parties. Do you feel this is the case in the "black market for computer cash," where presumably actual money changes hands? What, if anything, is

wrong with these voluntary transactions in your view?

7. Suppose dorm rooms were allocated by a "room draw" mechanism, where students picked a number and then chose rooms based on these numbers—e.g., lowest number got first choice, etc.

   a. Once rooms had initially been allocated in this fashion, would you be in favor of allowing "voluntary exchanges" (trades)? Why or why not?

   b. What about voluntary exchanges with "side payments" involving actual money? Why or why not?

   c. Would you be in favor of simply auctioning off dorm rooms to the highest bidder? Why or why not?

   d. Explain the difference between these last two mechanisms. *Hint:* Refer to your answers to questions 5a and 5b above.

8. Some schools offer computer time to their students "free of charge."

   a. How do you think computer facilities get paid for?

   b. A problem with "free" computer time is that the system gets overcrowded during "prime time." The result is often "rationing by waiting."

      (1) Why is "rationing by waiting" wasteful?

      (2) Propose a market-oriented approach for allocating peak period computer time.

      (3) What are some of the advantages/disadvantages of your proposal compared with "rationing by waiting"?

This article deals with such fundamental economic issues as economic versus free goods, market versus nonmarket rationing of a scarce good, and opportunity cost. It discusses the fact that at current (legal) prices, there is an economic shortage of healthy, white babies for adoption, leading to the existence of an illegal market. This shortage has increased due to factors that have shifted the supply curve in recent years. The last question accompanying the article examines the effects of price ceilings using supply and demand curves and should only be attempted after these curves have been introduced.

Price for Babies Rising in Wider Black Market

LOS ANGELES, April 24 (AP)—Babies are being sold in a fast-growing black market that charges anywhere from $5,000 for an illegal adoption to $50,000 for a custom-made child.

Healthy white infants have become such a profitable commodity in the United States that law enforcement officials fear the Mafia will soon become involved.

"It's a racket very susceptible to organized crime," said Deputy District Attorney Richard Moss of Los Angeles. He said there already seems to be a "loosely connected organization of child traffickers cooperating with each other in transporting babies across state lines."

Some states say they are dusting off ancient anti-slavery statutes to combat the flourishing people trade. Others are waiting for Senator Walter F. Mondale's subcommittee on children and youth to come up with Federal legislation.

Meanwhile, baby brokers are taking advantage of gray areas and loopholes in state adoption laws. And they are profiting because the demand for a certain type of baby exceeds the supply.

"We're going through an incredible, nationwide baby hunger at a time when adoptable infants are becoming scarce," said Charlotte DeArmond of the California Children's Home Society.

There is no shortage of children as such. Illegitimate births are at an all-time high of more than 400,000 a year, and the United States Department of Health, Education and Welfare says 120,000 children are available "for whom adoption would be best."

But they are either too old, the wrong color, or afflicted with muscular dystrophy, cerebral palsy or various psychological ailments. Selective foster parents are lining up for another kind of child: white, newborn, healthy and unwanted.

[A] Changing social mores, improved contraceptives, liberalized abortion laws and society's fading disapproval of unwed mothers makes this child a rarity. Thus he has become a prime target of black marketeers.

"The waiting list for white babies is now three to five years, while you can get a black baby in nine months," said Mrs. DeArmond.

Joseph Reid of the Child Welfare League of America said legitimate adoption agencies simply cannot compete with unscrupulous profiteers who offer pregnant girls large sums of money and pay all the medical bills for healthy white babies.

"Potatoes or babies, whenever a shortage develops a black market is going to fill the void," he said.

Children's agency officials estimate that one baby is sold on the black market for every 20 who find a home through legal adoption procedures. Mr. Moss said Californians, who have the reputation for being trailblazers in bizarre consumer trends, have done so in the baby-selling area too.

One California mother once gave her baby to a broker for a used car, and a childless couple paid $50,000 for a baby "made to order," selecting the parents from photographs of attractive, young, single men and women in an album compiled by their lawyer.

Some lawyers have placed classified ads in California newspapers ("Young people wish to adopt baby at birth. Will pay doctor and hospital bills. Replies confidential") and others are paying finders fees to college students for every pregnant coed they find on campus.

Mr. Moss said he is keeping watch on such developments in his state; but said he is powerless to prosecute for lack of evidence.

"The mother who sells her child won't talk because she's been paid off," he said. ■

QUESTIONS

1. Are "children" who are available for adoption "economic goods"? What about "healthy, white babies"? Explain with reference to the information in this article.

2. What is the "cost" of obtaining a healthy, white baby legally? What about obtaining such a baby in the "illegal market"? *Hint:* use the concept of opportunity cost.

3. Economic activity can be organized through either a "market mechanism" or a "nonmarket mechanism." If markets for healthy, white babies were legal, how would the allocation of this good differ from the current mechanism? In your answer, be sure to indicate what you think the current mechanism actually is.

4. **a.** Diagram what you think the demand curve for healthy, white babies looks like. Briefly explain your diagram.

   b. Do the same thing for the supply curve of healthy, white babies. Briefly explain your diagram.

   c. Explain why an "economic shortage" of healthy, white babies exists, and indicate this shortage on your diagram.

   d. Refer to passage A: Show the effect of the changes cited in the passage on your diagram from part **b** above, and also explain their effect on the size of the shortage.

   e. Do you think there would be an "economic shortage" of healthy, white babies if they could legally be bought and sold? Why or why not?

This article demonstrates that economic analysis can be useful in completely altering the way to view an issue. The author makes a major analytical error when he compares the salary of a draftee in West Germany with that of a U.S. Army voluntary enlistee to support his claim that the draft is "cheaper" than an all-volunteer army. The author also favors the draft on the basis of a debatable claim that the United States cannot meet its manpower goals under the all-volunteer army. Finally, the author raises the "moral" question of which policy—the draft or the all-volunteer army–would be of greater benefit to the poor and minorities. Once again, the author's conclusion is in direct contrast to the one provided using economic analysis.

Back to the Draft: It's More Economical, and It's Right

By JODY POWELL

If President Reagan should be so bold as to mention to any of our European allies their relatively low level of defense spending, he will be certain to hear at least one effective rejoinder.

Helmut Kohl and Francois Mitterand will remind him that those comparisons are flawed becaue West Germany and France, like most of our allies in the North Atlantic Treaty Organization, use conscription to fill out the ranks of their armed forces while the United States still relies on that flawed relic of Vietnam, the all-volunteer Army.

Meanwhile, back in the States, Sen. Ernest (Fritz) Hollings (D–S.C.) has once again introduced legislation to re-institute the draft. As in previous years, neither he nor anyone else really expects anything to come of it.

But he does it anyway, because he thinks that it's right and because he thinks that the time is drawing nigh when we will be forced to address the issues that he has been talking about since 1973, the year in which the all-volunteer force was established.

The man has a point.

[A] We still face the absolute certainty that the casualties in any future combat will come disproportionately from those in our society who get the least from it—the poor and minorities, particularly blacks.

Last year one-quarter of all new recruits were black, more than double their percentage in the population of the country. And the inequity is even greater in

armor, infantry and artillery—where casualties are always the highest.

"A free society defended by the least free," as Hollings puts it in his usual pungent fashion.

Those philosophical arguments have always been, and will remain valid. But they have also been, and are likely to remain, insufficiently persuasive. On this issue, appeals to the patriotism of the supposedly conservative collegians of today experience no more success than did appeals to the social conscience of their supposedly liberal predecessors.

[B] What is changing, and what bodes well to bring the issue to a head, are the practical considerations.

First there is the matter of demographics. "The baby boom is history," as Hollings points out. Which means that the pool from which the military does its recruiting is shrinking yearly.

In 1980 there were 11 million American males aged 17 to 21. In 1990 there will be fewer than 9 million.

In 1980 our manpower goals required the enlistment of one-fourth of those eligible; now it is two-fifths. By some estimates we will need one-half in 1993.

The fact is that we will not be able to do it. Though we are meeting recruiting goals at the moment, a combination of the shrinking pool and the expanding economy has already produced signs of trouble.

The military's Delayed Entry Program, which is generally considered to be the best indicator of recruiting potential, is lagging. Compared to the first five months of 1984, the program has experienced a drop-off of 19% this year.

The other inescapable fact is that the attempt to recruit an all-volunteer Army in the 1990s will be frightfully expensive.

[C] If Reagan wants to press his discussion with Kohl and Mitterrand, he will learn that they spend considerably less of their military budgets on salaries than we do. He will learn, for example, that a West German draftee's salary is 4,000 marks per year—about $1,300 at today's exchange rate—compared with $6,900 per year for an American recruit. (There are, of course, factors that narrow the contrast, but not enough to eliminate it.)

If the President had quizzed David A. Stockman on his recent diatribe against military retirement and other personnel benefits, his budget director would have been forced to admit that a significant factor in those rapidly escalating costs is the necessity of increasing benefits to attract a sufficient number of volunteers.

In the 1980s we are attempting to do as a society what was left to individuals in the 1860s: the hiring of substitutes to fight and die for the wealthy and priviledged.

By any standard of morality that attempt is an abomination. Practically it is working at the moment, but just barely. Hollings thinks that the budget squeeze may one day soon force us to do in the name of economy what we are unwilling to do simply because it's right. I for one hope that he turns out to be correct.

QUESTIONS

1. Consider passage C and assume the numbers cited are correct:
   a. How would you describe in words the economic cost (opportunity cost) of obtaining a military recruit?
   b. Use a production possibilities curve to illustrate your answer to part **a**, with the two goods being "military preparedness" and "all other goods."
   c. For which method is the economic cost of obtaining a given level of military preparedness lower, the draft or the all-volunteer army? Explain your reasoning.
   d. According to Powell, which method of obtaining our military manpower needs (the draft or the all-volunteer army) is cheaper? What accounts for the difference, if any, between your answer in part c and Powell's?
2. Refer to passage B, where Powell argues that it may become increasingly difficult to meet our current military recruiting goals under the all-volunteer army:
   a. Why would an "expanding economy" produce "signs of trouble" in this regard? *Hint:* Think about opportunity cost again.
   b. Do you feel the difficulty Powell cites is a valid argument in favor of the draft over the all-volunteer army? Explain your answer.
   c. Suppose it becomes necessary to increase the fringe benefits (or base salary for that matter) under the all-volunteer army in order to attract enough recruits to meet our military manpower goals. Would this mean that the economic cost of the all-volunteer army *relative* to the draft had increased? Why or why not? *Hint:* Think about the opportunity cost of obtaining a military recruit and refer to your production possibilities curve diagram.
3. Consider passage A:
   a. Under which policy—the draft or the all-volunteer army—do you think a poor person is worse off? Explain your reasoning carefully and make explicit any assumptions you are making in your answer.
   b. How does your answer compare with Powell's in this regard? Explain.
   c. Throughout U.S. history, the poor and minorities have been overrepresented in the military under both the draft and the all-volunteer army. Does this fact affect your answer above? Explain.

The common confusion between a "shift of" and a "movement along" a demand curve is readily apparent in this article about the response of European drivers to rising gasoline prices. The title of the article implies that gasoline is an exception to the "law of demand," but a proper classification of a number of events reported in the article leads to a different explanation of the behavior of European drivers.

Europe's Drivers Don't Reduce Gasoline Use Despite Soaring Prices

By JUNE KRONHOLZ

PARIS—Since the 1973–74 Arab oil embargo, the price of gasoline in France has almost tripled to the equivalent of $3.17 a gallon. The cost of running even a small car on the scale of Renault's Le Car adds up to 45 cents a mile. And filling up the tank of a big Citroen costs about $61.

So if price is a factor in the conservation of gasoline, as many energy-policy people in the U.S. believe, Frenchmen must be abandoning their cars by the garageful, *vrai?*

Faux. In fact, there are 22% more cars on the roads of France today than there were before the embargo. Gasoline and diesel-fuel consumption was up by 21% last year over 1973. The average French driver is putting 8,400 miles a year on his car, up from 7,800 in 1973. And 1.2 million cars fight their way into Paris every working day, making *l'embouteillage*—the bottle neck, as the French call their traffic jams—as much a part of the landscape as the Eiffel Tower.

Across Europe, motor-fuel consumption is increasing despite prices that are about double those in the U.S. Between 1976 and 1979, consumption of gasoline and diesel fuel rose by about 16% in West Germany and 10% in Britain. Between 1977 and 1979, automobile ownership increased by 10% in Belgium and Italy, by 12% in Austria and by 13% in Germany and Norway. Meanwhile, gasoline is selling for the equivalent of $2.32 for a U.S. gallon in London, $2.45 in Frankfurt, $2.53 in Geneva and $2.90 in Brussels.

Europe's experience is instructive for those who believe that gasoline consumption and auto use will fall as gasoline prices climb: In Europe, at least, the theory doesn't seem to work. "The French cannot imagine life without their car, whatever it costs them," says Louis Leger, director of L'Argus, a French newspaper devoted to the automobile industry. "The rest of Europe feels pretty much the same way."

But consider the recent experience in the U.S.: Gasoline prices have nearly doubled since the beginning of 1979, consumption declined 5% last year fom 1978, and so far this year consumption is down by 8%. Doesn't that show a link between price and consumption?

Energy analysts at the International Energy Agency, or IEA, an organization of 22 Western oil-importing countries, point out that U.S. drivers still burn up between three and four times as much gasoline as do drivers in France, Britain and Germany. Thus, Americans have more opportunities to eliminate gasoline waste than do Europeans.

A Long Way to Go

The U.S., analysts say, still has a long way to go before reaching the degrees of fuel efficiency that are common in Europe, and the decline in U.S. consumption also can be accounted for by such things as efforts to make cars more efficient, a slowing in the number of cars being added to the country's already huge fleet and a greater use of mass transportation.

European cars are thought to be about as small and as light, and therefore as fuel-efficient, as they can be—the biggest Saab gets 33 miles to the gallon and the smallest Volkswagen, 48. Europeans already make good use of mass transit. Having done about all they can to conserve through efficiency, Europeans clearly aren't prepared to cut back on gasoline consumption simply because of the price.

"We've concluded that price isn't effective in conservation," says Claude Thierry, an oil expert at the French industry ministry. "It might stun people momentarily, but the effect doesn't last." Indeed, a recent poll found Frenchmen declaring that gasoline would have to cost from six to 10 francs a liter—a staggering $5.25 to $8.70 a gallon—before they would change their driving habits.

Learning to Bear It

But how do Europeans afford gasoline that already is between $1 and $2 a gallon more than U.S. motorists are paying? The answer is by driving small cars, by charging cars to business expense accounts, by working and shopping close to home, and, as Americans are learning to do, by grinning and bearing it.

"So a tankful of gas costs 120 francs (about $30)—it costs that to go to dinner," says Gilbert Greenall, a young Paris businessman.

The French own about as many cars, pay about as much to operate them and are as passionate about driving as anyone else in Europe. Thus, a close look at what makes Pierre speed along provides some understanding of why it is so difficult to reduce gasoline consumption substantially.

France doesn't have any petroleum deposits of its own, and it imports all of its crude oil—91% from members of the Organization of Petroleum Exporting Countries. Gasoline prices have always been considerably higher in France than in the U.S. partly due to high taxes, which have provided the government with an important source of revenue. About 68% of the pump price of gasoline in France is tax, compared with about 10% in the U.S. The nearly $1.30 a gallon that American motorists are bewailing is incomprehensible to Frenchmen, who were paying $1 a gallon back in 1960.

"Americans have this attitude about the right to low-cost gas," says John Hemphill, an American who is an IEA administrator. "That attitude doesn't exist in Europe."

Gasoline prices in France remained fairly steady until 1974 when OPEC's increases in the price of crude oil caused the French pump price to jump by 40%. Since then, further increases have been frequent, although mostly small: 2% in February, 1977; 2% that June; 2% the following February; 11% in June, 1978, and 2% again in January, 1979. But after that, prices soared by 32%, or 77 cents a gallon.

"Gasoline always was high, but it went up gradually," says Susan Torn, a Paris writer who drives a British-made Austin. "It was easily absorbable in our budget."

[A] As gasoline prices were rising, so were hourly wages—by about 15% a year since 1974. Moreover, while prices at French gas pumps increased by 120% between 1973 and 1979, the real price, taking France's annual inflation rate of over 9% into account, increased just 23%, L'Argus estimates. Likewise, in Germany pump prices increased by 36% over the years while the real price went up only 3.7%, the IEA says. And in Britain, where pump prices soared by 120%, the real price actually fell by 8%.

Even though last year's OPEC price increases caused European pump prices to soar, the increases didn't hit as painfully as those in the U.S., where Washington's phasing out of price controls on domestic oil production pushed prices even higher. So although the price of gasoline increased, the French apparently never saw that as a reason to cut consumption permanently. Gas use did drop after the 1974 round of increases, but it began to rise again the next year and has been going up an average of 3.3% a year ever since.

The major reason for the rise in consumption here is simply that there are more cars than ever on French roads. Frenchmen bought two million new cars in 1978, the newspaper L'Argus says, despite a 33% luxury tax that pushes the current price of the cheapest Volkswagen to about $8,000 and of a five-passenger Peugeot 604 to about $20,000. There is now a passenger car for every three people in France. That is low compared with the U.S., where every other person owns a car, but high by world standards: one in four people owns a car in Britain, one in six in Japan and one in seven in Spain.

The Company Car

A company car and the cost of its upkeep are becoming key demands of European managers and many white-collar workers. About one-sixth of the late-model cars on French roads are company-owned, L'Argus estimates. In Britain, companies bought 43% of the new cars sold last year.

Nor has auto ownership approached the saturation point in Europe as many people think it has in the U.S. "Europeans are farther down the curve in auto ownership," the IEA's Mr. Hemphill says. "So it isn't a question of whether ownership will increase, but how fast."

[B] In addition to owning more cars than ever, Frenchmen are driving them more often. "A car no longer is the beautiful toy it was even 10 years ago," says Nicolas Crespelle, director of marketing research for Publics Conseil, an advertising agency that works for Renault. "It is now a tool of everyday life." Indeed, almost half the car owners in France regularly drive to work, despite bus and subway systems that would make commuting by public transit a good deal cheaper.

Then, too, the French are beginning to emulate the American life style that depends so heavily on the car: a house in the suburbs, shopping centers miles from home, weekends in the country. The Sunday drive is a major form of recreation; half of all French car owners claimed in a recent poll that they regularly go out on Sundays. Three out of every four also take to the roads for their government-legislated month-long vacations.

More Diesels

Even so, the French are making some adjustments. **[C] To take advantage of lower-priced diesel fuel (about $2 a gallon), the French owned 610,000 diesel-powered cars as of last year, triple the diesel ownership in 1974.**

The country's first speed limits were imposed after the 1973 embargo, although they were set so high—80 miles an hour on national highways—that they don't really promise much in the way of conservation.

[D] Mass transit is winning over more riders. Ridership on Paris buses, subways and trains has been rising since the embargo began the spiral in gasoline prices. Ridership had been steadily falling before then.

Plans to scrap more than a quarter of France's railroad track have been largely abandoned, and some new rail service has begun. Public transit systems are sprouting in smaller cities. For example, Caen, some-thing of a showcase for French mass-transit planners, has 134 miles of bus routes now compared with only 25 miles before the embargo.

But there are limits to how much the French can or will do to cut consumption. Most of the country's buses and subways are too crowded to be an attractive alternative to driving: Four people share every square yard of space on Parisian subway cars. The French government's interest in improving public transit is still only minimal. In 1978, the Interior Department says, France gave only $13 million to her cities to help buy public transit systems and equipment, compared with $105 million for work on city streets.

Overall, it can be said that French drivers seem pretty unconcerned about conservation. The French Communist Party recently started a poster campaign aimed at discouraging gasoline consumption. The campaign received such a listless reception that the Communists abandoned their effort even before they finished hanging all their posters. ∎

QUESTIONS

1. Draw the French demand curve for gasoline implied by the first three paragraphs of this article.
2. Consider the perspective of the article's typical French driver (Pierre), and decide whether each of the passages labeled A to D in the article reflects
   a. A movement along the demand curve for gasoline (a change in quantity demanded)
   b. A shift of the demand curve for gasoline (a change in demand)
3. Do French automobile drivers really violate the "law of demand," buying more gasoline in response to its higher price? If so, explain why. If not, explain what you think has really happened.

This article illustrates why the distinction between a "shift of" and a "movement along" a demand curve is so crucial. The title might initially lead one to ask what is wrong here, but the article goes on to describe three events that reconcile the title with the "law of demand."

The Price of Beer Rises at a Heady Pace, But Americans Are Thirstier Than Ever

By DAVID P. GARINO

ST. LOUIS—Beer, one of the few retail bargains in recent years, is joining the inflation trend.

Confronted by unprecedented cost increases, brewers are raising prices at a heady pace. Since the first of the year, wholesale prices on the average have gone up 6.6%, and further increases are expected. In contrast, wholesale prices the previous 10 years rose at an annual average rate of less than 1.5%.

The wholesale price increases are showing up in even larger markups at the retail level. One retailer here says he's selling Budweiser and Schlitz at $1.59 for a six-pack, which is up nearly 15% from $1.39 last summer. Though beer prices vary from market to market, in part reflecting competitive pressures and varying state excise taxes, it's clear that the familiar "week-end special" 99-cent six-pack is rapidly disappearing. "More price increases will be needed," says August A. Busch III, president of Anheuser-Busch Inc., the industry leader. Robert A. Uihlein Jr., chairman and president of Jos. Schlitz Brewing Co., flatly forecasts further price increases this year.

Brewers, as well as wholesalers, have viewed the price moves anxiously, fearing a slowdown in consumption. But beer drinkers are undeterred, quenching their thirsts at a faster pace. The U.S. Brewers Association reports that first-half shipments rose 5.6% to a record 72 million barrels. Indications are that July was a banner month. Anheuser-Busch, operating seven days a week, 24 hours a day, says July was the biggest month ever. Schlitz says its July volume increased "well above 10%," and Pabst Brewing Co. volume climbed 37%. Falstaff Brewing Co. volume was up 7%.

No Deals Any More

Price promotions also have decreased significantly from last year. Eugene C. Weissman, who heads Pet Inc.'s chain of retail liquor stores, recalls that in 1973 discounts were offered with the wholesale purchase of 50 to 100 cases of beer. "Now, no one is offering us any deals," he observes.

Beer companies say that not only are the price increases cost-justified, but they are long overdue. Even after brewers received Cost of Living Council permission to hike prices last year, competition restrained such action. "Brewers were getting killed by higher costs, and eventually they had to raise prices," says Donald Rice, a securities analyst at Frederick & Co. in Milwaukee. For instance, Pabst recently reported that first-half profits plunged to $6.5 million, or 71 cents a share, from $14.2 million, or $1.50 a share, the year before.

Principal cost pressures have been felt in commodities and packaging, particularly cans. Barley is now approaching $4 a bushel, compared with $1.20 a year ago, with some predictions that it will reach $4.50 later this year. Thomas A. Nelson, a vice president and analyst at Robert W. Baird & Co. of Milwaukee, points out, "Each crop forecast from the Department of Agriculture shows a downward revision. That's the stuff of which higher prices are made." Another analyst, Andrew Melnick, a vice president at Drexel, Burnham & Co. in New York, sees the crop situation contributing to still higher beer prices in 1975. "Once a crop is harvested, you have to wait till next year for any improvement," he notes. "You can't produce corn or barley from nothing."

Falstaff's "Treadmill"

On the packaging side, Falstaff has been hit with four can-price increases totaling 35% this year. "We're on a treadmill," says Fred J. Gutting, chairman and president. "No sooner do we try to recover part of our costs with a price increase than we get another increase from our suppliers."

There are practically as many theories as there are beer drinkers to account for the strong demand even in the face of higher prices. One involves the weather. Brewers say that torrid temperatures in July boosted sales. "Mr. Sun is still our best salesman," says a spokesman for F. & M. Schaefer Co.

Another common explanation for lack of consumer resistance is that beer prices haven't gone up as fast as many others. "Beer is still a hell of a good buy," says Orion P. Burkhardt, a vice president of Anheuser-Busch. "Everything is going up at the supermarket, and consumers are much smarter than some people give them credit for. They can readily see that when cooking oil goes from 90 cents to $1.10 a bottle, that's a bigger percentage increase than when a six-pack goes from $1.49 to $1.59."

Beer executives also point out that in some markets soft drinks cost as much as or even more than beer.

In addition, the market has been broadened. In the past three years, 20 states have lowered the legal drinking age to 18 and the number of "dry" areas has been continually reduced, says Phil Katz, research vice president for the brewers association.

The College Market

Beer companies also sense that there is more interest in beer drinking on college campuses as students turn away from marijuana and hard drugs. Miller Brewing Co., a unit of Philip Morris Inc., recently appointed a manager of college marketing to push sales to students. Schaefer has shifted its advertising theme to include more young people in contemporary settings.

Even though people are buying more beer, brewers are aware there may be a price at which consumers will start to balk. "How far is up? No one knows for sure," one brewery executive says. But Jerry Steinman, who publishes a beer-industry newsletter, notes that "in some Southern states where there are high excise taxes, six-packs are selling for well over $2 and yet business is booming."

Brewers are taking some steps to offset higher costs. Anheuser-Busch has eliminated the two-day setting period in its brewing process, which the company says doesn't hinder quality but increases capacity. Falstaff in the past year has slashed $1.8 million from its marketing, administrative and general expenses. Schlitz committed $100 million for three new can plants, so that by the 1980s the company will be making 75% to 80% of its cans. Schlitz's Mr. Uihlein estimates that this will save the company $6 per thousand cans. ∎

QUESTIONS

1. According to the title of this article, what has happened to the price of beer? To the quantity consumed?
2. According to the article, brewers and wholesalers had feared that the price increases would result in a slowdown in consumption.
   a. Why do you think this did not occur?
   b. How, if at all, can you reconcile what did occur with the "law of demand"?
3. Which of the following events cited in this article are consistent with the changes in the price and quantity of beer indicated by the title of the article? Justify your answer in each case with an appropriate diagram showing how the particular event affected the beer market.
   a. The costs of barley and packaging (beer cans) have increased.
   b. Beer prices have not gone up as fast as many other prices, such as those of soft drinks.
   c. During the past three years, twenty states have lowered the legal drinking age to eighteen, and the number of "dry" areas has continually been reduced.
   d. Torrid temperatures occurred in July 1974.

It is easier to appreciate a market equilibrium after examining a disequilibrium. This article about thirty thousand job applicants lining up for 350 new unionized longshore personnel positions provides a colorful example of a market disequilibrium outside the typical context of government price controls.

Wheeling for Wages

By JUDY PASTERNAK

Lines of job seekers in cars, vans and Jeeps—even an ice cream truck—extended for 10 miles when a makeshift drive-through employment office in an industrial section of San Pedro opened at 7 a.m. Sunday.

By the time the "office" at the San Pedro Drive-in closed at 5 p.m., about 30,000 applications—for 350 dock-workers' jobs—had been distributed by union and port employers' representatives.

Vehicles had begun lining up near the drive-in at noon Friday, in response to advertisements and media announcements that the applications would be handed out Sunday. Hundreds—mostly residents of communities near the harbor—spent most of the weekend sitting in lawn chairs on curbs, listening to portable radios, barbecuing meals on hibachis and meeting up unexpectedly with old friends.

They didn't need to discuss why they wanted one of the waterfront jobs. When asked, their responses rarely varied: even those already employed were willing to wait for a chance at the $15.57-per-hour base pay for lifting and lashing boxes, crates and sacks or for checking the cargo inside.

"This is good pay," said Marcus Cahill, a 25-year-old jewelry salesman and the driver of a silver BMW carrying four passengers—the first carload to receive application forms as police waved traffic through a checkpoint on Gaffey Street outside the drive-in at 7 a.m.

Said Chris Carino, a 26-year-old truck driver at the harbor, who was farther back in line: "I already work at the port, but I make $7.35 an hour. There's no comparison." Like Cahill, he is a San Pedro resident.

The applications were in such demand that some drivers at the head of the line were able to sell places in their vehicles. Johnny Quesada, a 21-year-old from Bell, said he paid $10 to ride in a stranger's truck.

There also was a marketplace for the forms themselves. Said Mary Ann Migehino, of Brennan, Wash.: "Way, way back (in line), somebody offered me $50 for my application."

The distribution was largely peaceful, marred only by a skirmish about five minutes after the start, when a pick-up truck jammed with 33 passengers was handed just 30 applications.

Each vehicle was directed through one of four lanes, marked by orange cones or poles, where members of a joint union-employers group stood with cartons of the seven-page application forms.

The last mass dock-workers' hiring was in 1980, when 15,000 applied for about 500 jobs, said Charlie Young, labor relations representative for the employers' group, an organization of stevedoring companies called the Pacific Maritime Assn.

Since then, employment has remained steady at about 2,600. But in the last six months, business has boomed at the adjoining Los Angeles–Long Beach ports. They combine to make up the fastest-growing waterfront in the world, industry experts say. General cargo volume is up 12.5% over last year at Los Angeles; it has increased by 11.3% in Long Beach.

But the result is a labor shortage that has kept ships waiting in port for days to load or unload. With operating costs ranging from $10,000 to $30,000 a day, shipping companies are not happy about the delays.

Those who received applications must return the filled-out forms, along with a $5 processing fee, to the San Pedro Drive-in from 9 a.m. to 3 p.m today, Tuesday or Wednesday.

About 700 of the applicants will be interviewed in November for the dockworker positions, said Terry Lane, the association's assistant area manager for Southern California. By December, hiring should be complete, he said.

The International Longshoremen's and Warehousemen's Union and the employers have not yet agreed on a scoring system to rank applicants, Lane said. Because of a 1982 settlement of a federal court lawsuit, about 30% of the jobs will go to women, Lane said.

Applications will remain on file for a year; several hundred more dockworkers will be hired if the labor crunch does not ease, he added.

Lane and Young said they were surprised by the numbers that turned out. "We had about 20,000 applications prepared, with everyone filling out a duplicate form," Lane said. "But when we heard about the lines over the weekend, we decided not to have duplicates and that doubled how many forms we had on hand."

As the distribution began, police said, two lines of vehicles extended for about 5 miles each, and most of them had been there at least overnight. The Friday and Saturday night revelers "woke me up outside my house four miles away," said Dave Miller, ILWU Local 63's president.

Ashraf Mohammed, night cashier at a Thrifty Gas Station about 5 miles from the drive-in, said more than 100 cars pulled up to the pumps from midnight to 6 a.m. Sunday. "They don't want gas. All they want to know is where is this San Pedro Drive-In," he said.

He wondered why they were looking for the place, and when he was told, Mohammed plucked a piece of paper out of his shirt pocket. "What is the address?" he asked.

Many of the early arrivals parked their vehicles to reserve a place and left. "Nobody could cut in line," said Saul Godoy, 33. "It was bumper to bumper."

Godoy and three friends were to meet Sunday with another man who had parked his truck in the line Friday night. But the man did not show up Sunday. "We had no keys," Godoy said.

The truck behind them pushed their vehicle along for ¾ of a mile to the checkpoint, Godoy said. The man who didn't appear "doesn't get an application," he added.

Others did not want to wait patiently. Jim Myers of Long Beach and Alan Fry, who traveled 10 hours from Sacramento, cut into the line on their motorcycles. Lloyd Ricks, 30, of San Pedro, drove his four-wheel drive car over nearby railroad tracks to get past police directing traffic.

By 10 a.m., there was little need for such tactics. Kim Falaniko, a 27-year-old aerobics instructor from Harbor City who emerged past the checkpoint about that time, said she had not arrived until 8:30 a.m.

"I told my friends to come in the afternoon," said the Pacific Maritime Assn.'s Young. "That way, they could just drive right up." ∎

QUESTIONS

1. Draw supply and demand curves for new longshore personnel, and use your diagram to depict the current situation in the market. Use numbers from the article to specifically label the current wage rate and the quantities of new applicants demanded and supplied.

2. Consider the current disequilibrium situation in the new longshore personnel market:
   a. What wage adjustment is necessary to help bring this market into equilibrium?
   b. What single piece of evidence from the article most convinces you that a wage adjustment may be in order?
   c. Would you expect market forces to exert pressure to bring about your suggested wage adjustment? If not, why not? If so, what keeps wages from adjusting?

This article discusses a variety of events that influence demand and supply in the domestic mink market. The article has been around awhile, but it provides an unusually straightforward and complete set of supply and demand examples. Passages from the article illustrate changes in tastes, income, price of substitutes, technology, input costs, and number of producers.

Mink Farming Is Growing More Scarce as Costs Rise and Fur Demand Declines

By MICHAEL L. GECZI

NEW YORK—Mink farms could well be on the endangered-species list.

The animals themselves never have reached an endangered status, but the number of U.S. farms raising the small mammals for their pelts has decreased sharply in recent years.

[A] In the industry's peak year, 1966, about 6,000 mink farms were operating in the U.S. Today, there are 1,221 according to the U.S. Agriculture Department.

Despite slight increases the past two years, total pelt production last year was 3.1 million, or half of the record 6.2 million pelts produced in 1966. Annual sales at the auction level, where most pelts are sold, were about $54 million in 1974, according to one estimate, down from more than $120 million in the mid-1960s.

The smaller operations have been the hardest hit. "The mom and pop outfits and the part-timers were the ones that folded," says an Agriculture Department official. "The bigger farms have kept operating."

Some industry officials say a profitable mink farm of any size is rare. "We've been in dire straits for the past four or five years," says Robert Langenfeld, president of Associated Fur Farms Inc., New Holstein, Wis., one of the nation's largest mink farms.

[B] The industry's descent has been as rapid as its rise in the 1950s and 1960s, during which time mink grew in popularity as a fashionable status symbol. Growth was aided by the development of new colors (there are currently 13). As producers' feed and labor costs remained relatively stable in the face of strong demand, more people entered the industry.

Unsold Inventories

Growth proved to be too rapid, however; large unsold inventories from the record 1966 crop caused a price bust in 1967, and the situation has worsened since. **[C] Feed and labor costs have climbed rapidly. [D] Competition from less-expensive foreign pelts has heightened.**

Perhaps most important, mink has lost much of its prestige. Industry officials say the desire to wear a mink coat has in many instances given way to ecological concerns. Cries from conservationists "caused a mass reaction for the 'poor animal,'" says Louis Henry, president of Hudson Bay Fur Sales Inc., The Hudson's Bay Co. unit that handles about two-thirds of the pelts sold at auction in the U.S. annually.

Mr. Henry recalls that in 1966 pelts sold at auction for an average of $24 each. The going price today for a mutation (colored) skin is about $14. Dark furs bring a slightly higher price.

In the 1960s, a mink producer would net about $5 on a mutation pelt, says Mr. Langenfeld. **[G]"Now," he says, "we're losing about $3 a pelt on our mutations." He says it costs the company $17 to raise a kit, or young mink, and bring its pelt to auction.**

Mink farmers breed their animals in March. The kits—usually four to a litter—are born in early May. They're raised for six months before being killed—humanely, producers say—by gas or electrocution. The skins then are removed and readied for sale.

Finicky Animal

In most cases they are sent to one of four main U.S. auction centers, in New York City, Seattle, Minne-

19

apolis and Milwaukee. Fees received by one of the two associations that offer the pelts for sale and by the company conducting the auction can take up to 7.75% of the pelt's selling price.

The price the producers get for their pelts is their reward for raising a finicky animal that prefers only the freshest meat, poultry and fish. Most mink farms have expensive refrigeration, grinding and mixing machines, and also must hire extra help to thaw and feed daily rations to the animals. All this causes the mink's diet to represent more than half of the total cost of raising a mink to pelt-producing size.

[E] Mink researchers have been working to develop a dry diet that would be more economical and still satisfy the taste and nutritional requirements of the animal. Some farmers are using the dry diets, but they are far from gaining industry-wide acceptance.

U.S. producers are said to produce a high-quality pelt much prized by those who don't mind paying handsomely for a coat or stole. But about half of the six million or so pelts used annually in the U.S. are less expensive than foreign ones produced mainly in Scandinavia. Some industry officials say an increasing number of garments made from these pelts are being sold to people who formerly would have bought the more expensive item made from U.S.-produced pelts.

Mr. Henry says the worst may be over, however. "I think it (sales) will stabilize just about where it is," he says. **[F] Some observers expect a pickup in business as the recession eases.**

Will business ever return to the good old days? "I don't know any mink farmers who ever had any good old days," says Mr. Langenfeld. ∎

QUESTIONS

1. Use supply and demand diagrams to illustrate the effects on equilibrium price and quantity in the domestic mink market that are implied by each of the passages labeled A to F. For passage E, depict the results of a successful research effort.

2. Taking passages C and D together, would the equilibrium quantity of domestic mink rise, fall, remain the same, or change in an uncertain direction? What about the equilibrium price of domestic mink?

This article traces the effects of an increase in the price of sugar in the moonshine market and then in a related market, the market for legal whiskey. It can also be used to review the relationship between changes in total revenue and the price elasticity of demand.

Moonshiners in South Find Sales Are Down as Their Costs Go Up

By JONATHAN KWITNY

My daddy, he made whiskey
My granddaddy did, too
We ain't paid no whiskey tax
Since 1792.

—from "Copper Kettle" by Albert F. Beddoe

HABERSHAM COUNTY, Ga.—When Joan Baez popularized the song "Copper Kettle" in the early 1960s, the verse quoted above described life in these North Georgia hills pretty accurately.

"There probably isn't a family around here that hasn't had at least one member involved with a still," observes Clyde Dixon, executive vice president of the Peoples Bank in Cleveland,Ga. "It hasn't been so long around here since moonshine was the only way to make money. My father made moonshine," Mr. Dixon says.

[A] But two years ago the price of sugar—an essential ingredient in moonshine—tripled, and life in the laurel thickets changed rapidly. It takes at least 10 pounds of sugar to make a gallon of barnyard whiskey. With other inflationary factors added, moonshine that sold a few years ago for $6 a gallon at the still began pushing $15 a gallon.

At that price the moonshine market contracted severely, because for $15 plus retail markup, a customer can buy government whiskey. ("Government whiskey" is the hill country term for legal booze—stuff on which the tax has been paid. Unlike hastily made moonshine, its manufacture relies on slowly drawing natural sugars from the grain being distilled, and therefore its price is unaffected by the sugar market.)

Revenuers Look Elsewhere

The price squeeze on moonshine has forced new occupations on a lot of people who were engaged, one way or another, in what may have been, even as late as the 1950s, the largest industry in such counties as Habersham, Dawson and Gilmer. Not all of those people whose employment depended on illegal booze were moonshiners, themselves, however.

Billy Corbin is a revenue agent with the Treasury Department's Bureau of Alcohol, Tobacco and Firearms (ATF). He chased moonshiners in North Georgia for 10 years and says his team of five agents used to bust up an average of 10 stills a month. Then, in December, he was transferred to a new office with emphasis on nonwhiskey violations. "When I left (the moonshine post) it was down to no more than one still a month," Mr. Corbin says.

Mr. Corbin's boss, Bill Barbary, agent in charge of ATF's Gainesville, Ga., office, says the 108 revenue agents in Georgia used to spend 75% of their time on liquor offenses, the rest on other crimes, mostly the unlicensed sale of firearms. Now, he says, agents spend only about 25% of their time on moonshine patrol. To help fill the slack, the Treasury Department this year reassigned its gambling tax enforcement to ATF from the Internal Revenue Service.

So, for the government, one beneficial by-product of the sugar inflation and moonshine depression is an increase in arrests for firearms violations and illegal wagering. Some 15 or 20 revenue agents from the countryside were reassigned to Atlanta this spring and broke up a big numbers ring there, federal officials say; they promise to follow up with the indictment of 30 or 40 gambling operators.

The Pot Shuttle

On the other hand, with the whiskey business in turmoil, many former moonshine overlords—Mr. Barbary says most of them—have simply reapplied their resourcefulness to trafficking in other illicit goods that are still profitable. They are suspected of being responsible for the recent big increase in the airlifting of drugs, particularly marijuana, from South America to small airstrips in Georgia and neighboring moonshine states.

For example, two long-reputed North Georgia moonshine czars, Garland "Bud" Cochran and Ben Kade "Junior" Tatum, were indicted in federal court in South Carolina last summer for allegedly masterminding a DC-4 pot shuttle from Colombia. Mr. Tatum was convicted and is appealing. Mr. Cochran—who the ATF says was shipping 7,000 gallons of moonshine a month into Atlanta in trailer trucks during the 1960s—has been a fugitive since the smuggling indictment came down. Officials believe he is in South America directing more smuggling operations.

Radical as the change in North Georgia life has been since the price of sugar rose, it actually is the culmination of an evolutionary change that began in the early 1940s.

> Get you a copper kettle
> Get you a copper coil
> Cover with new-made corn mash
> And never more you'll toil.

Revenue agents agree that the old-time, 100% corn liquor made in pure copper stills—the fabled "white lightning"—was as good as or better than bonded whiskey. But when copper became scarce at the start of World War II, moonshiners turned to sheet metal vats, and in more recent times began cooling the liquor in automobile radiators instead of copper coils. The result often is a fatal dose of lead poisoning. In probably the most famous case of this, the late Fats Hardy, a Gainesville moonshine king, was sentenced to life in prison in the late 1950s after many persons died from drinking the moonshine he shipped to Atlanta.

The people who do drink it, authorities say are almost exclusively poor, urban blacks. The biggest retail distribution centers are so-called "shot-houses," operated in private homes or stores in black neighborhoods of Atlanta, Macon and other cities throughout the Southeast. Because the price of a shot has soared to 75 cents, almost the price of safer, stronger legal bar whiskey, the ATF estimates that there are only a few hundred shot-houses in Atlanta now, down from a few thousand before the crunch.

Assistant U.S. Attorney Owen Forrester in Atlanta—who says his grandmother had a still on her land, though she didn't drink—says he doubts that even a new rise in sugar prices could wipe out moonshine entirely. "The revenue agents who work the shot-houses here tell me that there are still a lot of old-timers who like the taste of it," Mr. Forrester says. "There's a certain zang, or sizzle, going down."

How to Make It

Hill folks and revenue agents have described the methods moonshiners use to get that "zang" and "sizzle" in there.

First, there's a widespread belief, often put into practice, that horse manure added to the corn mash speeds its fermentation. In addition, sanitary conditions aren't always up to FDA standards. Mr. Dixon, the country banker, says. "I've seen a hog get in (the vat) to drink some of that slop and drown. They just take the hog out and go ahead. They can't afford to lose all that money (by throwing out the contaminated mash). I'll tell you, Jack Daniel's does it a lot cleaner." Mr. Forrester, the prosecutor, recalls a moonshiner who "put in dead possums at the end to flavor it."

Later, still other foreign matter is added. Moonshine usually is 110 proof when it's sold at the still to a "tripper," who usually is either an independent truck driver or an employee of an urban distributor. To stretch the product, the distributors usually water it down as much as 50%. Then, to make it look its original strength, they add beading oil, which simulates the swirls that alcohol makes in liquor.

If some parts of the "Copper Kettle" song were accurate once, sources here agree that one verse never was accurate:

> You just lay there by the juniper
> While the moon is bright
> And watch them jugs a-fillin'
> In the pale moonlight.

"It's damn hard work to make whiskey," Mr. Dixon says. "They have to hide the stills in laurel thickets on a mountain. You have your barrels and boxes of malt—it's corn meal mostly, some barley malt. They'll carry 200 or 300 pounds of sugar up that mountain at a time on their backs. All the time (the mash) is working it has to be stirred. That corn meal has a tendency to lump up. I've seen them get stark naked and get in there and mash it. If you don't think it's hard work, try it."

Much of the hard work, high price and poor quality is caused by the revenue agents, whose presence puts constant pressure on moonshiners to finish their work fast and get out. Moonshiners need costly sugar because they must dash off each batch of their product in about 72 hours. Bonded distillers have controlled conditions and plenty of time, so they can apply even heat as required and wait out the two weeks or so it takes to get sugar out of the natural grains.

> Build you a fire with hick'ry
> Hick'ry and ash and oak
> Don't use no green or rotten wood
> They'll get you by the smoke.

Byron Davis of Gainesville, who retired in 1968 after 31 years as a revenue agent because "it's a young man's job," says he remembers capturing a lot of moonshiners by cruising the hills looking for smoke. In fact, he attributes the switch in still materials from copper to other metals at least in part to a switch in cooking fuels from wood to butane gas. The butane largely eliminated the telltale smoke trail, he says, but didn't work well with copper equipment.

Keeping tabs on sugar sales also has helped agents to corral a few moonshiners. "One of these little country stores starts selling 500 pounds of sugar a week, you smell a rat,"Mr. Corbin says.

Nowadays, however, agents say they make most of their arrests through tips from informants. Moonshiners love to tell on each other, Mr. Corbin says. Certainly the ATF needed informants 18 months ago in order to discover a fabulous 2,000-gallon-a-week underground still, which was entered by opening the trunk of an old Ford sitting in a Habersham County junkyard, and climbing down a ladder. Agents believe that the operator obtained electric power for his still by tapping into nearby underground Tennessee Valley Authority lines.

On the whole, authorities say their problem is less in catching moonshiners than in obtaining justice afterwards.

Judges and juries just "didn't consider whiskey to be a crime," Mr. Forrester recalls of his moonshine trial days. The operator of the underground still beneath the old Ford, for example, pleaded guilty and received a suspended sentence, Mr. Forrester says.

Professional

So relaxed is the atmosphere at moonshine trials that one notorious moonshiner from Adairsville, Ga., used to feel comfortable attending them. Mr. Forrester recalls, "Every term he'd come to court with mash all over his pants and listen to testimony in other cases to learn new techniques."

A typical still operation is financed and overseen by a man with substantial income from legitimate business, such as a farm or store. He hires three to six still hands and one or two women who live with them while the still is in operation, to keep house and to make the group appear to be a normal family. While the still hands sometimes wind up serving a year or two in federal prison, the boss, if convicted, usually gets probation, often impressing the judge and jury with letters of commendation from leaders in the community. . . . ■

QUESTIONS

1. Consider passage A: Explain carefully (with the use of a supply and demand diagram) what is occurring in the market for moonshine.
2. Now indicate on a new diagram how the change in the moonshine market depicted above affects the market for legal whiskey.
3. The title of the article states: ". . . Sales Are Down As . . . Costs Go Up." If "sales" are defined as the total expenditure on moonshine, what, if anything, can you say about the price elasticity of demand for moonshine? Explain briefly.
4. Congress is considering raising the federal excise tax on government (legal) whiskey in order to reduce the federal deficit:
   a. Explain and then illustrate on a diagram how such a tax increase would affect the market for legal whiskey.
   b. Which, if any, of the following would make the price of legal whiskey rise by the full amount of the tax?
      (1) Horizontal demand and upward sloping supply
      (2) Vertical demand and upward sloping supply
      (3) Downward sloping demand and upward sloping supply
      (4) Downward sloping demand and horizontal supply
      (5) Downward sloping demand and vertical supply

This editorial about the consumer response to skyrocketing coffee prices makes a classic error. Can you find it?

Consumers and Coffee

Coffee prices, it seems, are coming down again, after hitting a record high of $4.42 last year. **[A] An Agriculture Department economist, who had predicted $5-a-pound coffee this year, says he "underestimated the power of the U.S. consumer movement."** Perhaps, or maybe, as with so many economists these days, he simply forgot his freshman economics, which has nothing to do with "movements." The coffee market is behaving the way the basic textbooks say a market behaves. Prices go up, demand falls, and prices come down. ■

QUESTIONS

1. Consider the last sentence of this editorial:
   a. Do you agree with this description of a market response to a decrease in the supply of coffee? Explain your reasoning carefully, making use of a supply and demand diagram.
   b. If you disagree, how would you alter the sentence to make it a valid statement of how markets behave when supply decreases?
2. Consider passage A: The "consumer movement" mentioned in this passage turns out to be attempts by various consumer groups to organize a "coffee boycott" by coffee drinkers to reduce the price of coffee.
   a. How would such a "boycott" by consumers affect a supply and demand diagram of the coffee market?
   b. Would your own individual decision to join the boycott affect the price of coffee? Explain.
   c. Suppose the boycott is initially "successful" and the price of coffee falls. If consumers now return to their old coffee-drinking habits, will the price of coffee remain at its new lower level? Explain.
   d. Use your answers to questions 2a, 2b, and 2c to explain why economists (like the one quoted in passage A) are generally pessimistic about the likely success of a consumer boycott in lowering prices.

Thinking of demand as a specific amount instead of a relationship between various prices and quantities demanded is a common and costly confusion when the market involves a "necessity" such as health care. This article about the market for doctors ignores the functional role of prices when discussing both an "oversupply" of doctors and a quantity of health care in "substantial excess of requirements" by the year 2000.

US Faces Oversupply of Doctors by 2000

WASHINGTON, D.C.—UPI—[A] America's supply of doctors could exceed demand by the year 2000, and already there are signs the number of doctor-short areas is shrinking, according to a Health and Human Services Department report.

"The best judgment is that the nation should have at least an adequate supply of physicians over the coming two decades," said the third report on health personnel in the United States.

[B] "By the year 2000, the supply of physicians is expected to be more than adequate to meet demand, and could very well be in substantial excess of requirements," it said.

The increased supply could lead to lower fees, shorter waiting times and better care in physician-short areas. But the report noted some experts believe an oversupply "could also have negative impacts, such as increasing unnecessary care."

There were nearly 450,000 active medical doctors and osteopaths in the United States in 1980, up 55.7% since 1965, the report said. Dentists numbered 126,000, up 31.4%; optometrists 22,300, up 28.9%; pharmacists 144,200, up 38.5%; podiatrists 8,900, up 17.1%; and veterinarians 36,000, up 54.5%.

"In 1980, the active supply in all of the health professions with which this report is concerned . . . stood at record levels, both in aggregate numbers and in the ratio of practitioners to population," the report said.

"For physicians, it appears that the trend toward a lesser supply in rural areas, which existed in the 1960s, has halted and perhaps even reversed in the 1970s; and there is evidence of increased location of medical specialists in rural areas."

Dentists are also moving to rural areas, as are physician assistants, a profession that did not exist in 1965 and now numbers 8,800, the report said.

But the report said there still were areas short of doctors, with no relief in sight.

Enrollment in health profession schools grew rapidly from the mid 1960s to the early 1970s. Although first-year enrollments are at a record high, they may be leveling off in podiatry and medicine and dropping in dentistry and pharmacy, the report said.

The number of applicants is down from the peak years of the mid–70's, with the largest percentage of the decline among white men, the report said.

Federal financial support has helped raise the number of women enrolled in health profession schools but has been less successful in raising minority enrollment, the report said.

Female enrollment ranges from 2.4 times the 1971 enrollment in pharmacy to 16.8 times in podiatry. Minority enrollment runs from 1.5 times the 1971 enrollment in pharmacy to four times the number in podiatry.

Women make up a significant proportion of the total enrollment in most health profession schools, ranging from 11% in schools of podiatry to 44% in pharmacy schools, the report said.

Minority enrollment, ranging from 4% in veterinary schools to 13% in medical schools, is nearly double what it was in the early 1970s but few gains have been made since the mid 1970s, the report said. Minority enrollment in US medical schools peaked at 6.3% in 1974–75, and has since dropped to 5.7%, the report said. ■

QUESTIONS

1. Use a supply and demand diagram to illustrate the major change that appears to be currently under way in the market for doctors.
2. The title suggests that the market for doctors will not be in equilibrium by 2000. Do you agree? Use your diagram from question 1 to support your answer, and be sure to label what you think is referred to by "oversupply of doctors."
3. The article consistently overlooks the functional role that prices can play in the health-care industry. What error is attributable to this oversight in passages A and B of the article?
4. Consider passage A:
   a. Draw a supply and demand diagram for doctor services for the year 2000 that is consistent with a literal interpretation of passage A.
   b. According to your diagram, what will be the price of doctor services in the year 2000?

Selection Twelve

This article complements the textbook analysis of rent control by providing a number of concrete details concerning the rent control experience of Santa Monica. The initial questions accompanying the article address efficiency issues: diagramming the basic situation, citing and classifying concrete examples of the effects of rent control in Santa Monica, and commenting on some specific provisions of rent control discussed in the article. Additional questions address equity issues: explaining the irony of the article's title, identifying the winners and losers from rent control, and explaining the "political economy" of how rent control persists in Santa Monica despite the many problems cited in the article.

Santa Monica—Only the Elite Need Apply

By ALAN CITRON

When the renters' "underground" alerted Melissa Clare to an apartment vacancy in Santa Monica, the free-lance writer assumed that her chances of getting into the embattled rent-control city were virtually nil.

Living within earshot of the ocean for $280 a month was an alluring proposition. In just three days, the owner of the vacant one-bedroom apartment had talked to more than 200 prospective tenants.

The fact that Clare eventually triumphed over the other applicants is credited to a strong recommendation from the outgoing tenant, a member of Clare's close-knit network of renter friends. Most people are not so lucky.

Five years after Santa Monica voters approved the nation's toughest and most controversial rent-control law—after the so-called "renter's revolt" put a lid on spiraling rents and demolitions—the city has experienced an unrelenting demand for apartments.

"If you find a place in Santa Monica you just move, no matter where you are," said the 26-year-old Clare. "You feel so fortunate to be living here. It's like a special club. . . . It's a sweet life."

The desirability of living in Santa Monica has not been lost on the city's apartment owners and developers. Bumper stickers that sarcastically welcomed visitors to the "People's Republic of Santa Monica" are no longer quite so visible. But the long-running feud between landlords and tenants—80% of Santa Monica's

residents live in apartments—continues to draw national attention to the city.

"Santa Monica has the most comprehensive rent-control law in the country," said John Gilderbloom, an urban studies professor at the University of Wisconsin–Green Bay and author of "Rent Control: A Source Book.

"Landlords are realizing that this is where the first battle has got to be pitched, that they have got to knock off this rent-control law because many communities are now trying to emulate it," Gilderbloom said.

Dramatic Effect on City

In its simplest form, rent control acts as a stabilizer on rapidly rising rents. Roughly half of the apartments in California and 10% of the apartments nationwide are covered by some form of rental regulation, according to urban planners. While Santa Monica's law has won the respect of people like Gilderbloom by tightly regulating rents and preventing demolitions, the effect on the city has been dramatic.

■ Finding an apartment in Santa Monica has become nearly impossible: It is not uncommon for upward of 400 people to apply for one vacancy, and some people have been on waiting lists for more than two years. Most apartment vacancies are not advertised. Of the ones that are, roughly two-thirds are rented through agencies that charge fees of as much as $1,000 for their services. Because the competition for apartments is so fierce, apartment owners said they most often choose as tenants young professionals who are more likely to pay for repairs and improvements to their units. While rent control was originally promoted as a way of keeping the city affordable, city planners have estimated that "Santa Monica today has fewer low- and moderate-income people than at any time in its recent history. . . ."

■ Maintenance of apartment buildings has declined: Many apartment owners, angry about low profits on their buildings, have decreased general maintenance. Maintenance-related complaints filed by tenants have more than doubled since the passage of rent control, according to the city's building and safety division.

■ Apartment building sales and construction remain in decline: **[A] Even though new buildings are exempt from rent control (except for units built under special government contracts), a minimal amount of apartment construction has taken place since rent control.** Apartment buildings are selling at an average of $200,000 less than market value in comparable areas and sales are sluggish, according to the Santa Monica Board of Realtors.

Expensive to Administer

✳ ■ Administering rent control is expensive. The city's rent-control budget exceeds $2.3 million and costs each tenant $72 a year in fees. On a per capita basis, it is by far the most expensive rent-control effort in the country.

Much of the cost is due to litigation. During the last five years, opponents have filed close to 300 lawsuits against the Santa Monica law, spending more than $1 million in the process. The board's legal staff spent about $700,000 defending rent control in fiscal 1983–84 alone. Berkeley's rent stabilization program, by comparison, has been sued about a dozen times in its 14-year history.

Ken Baar, a Berkeley attorney and nationally known rent-control consultant, contends that Santa Monica's law has come under such strong attack because of the beach community's lure for real estate developers. "Obviously the budget is high," Baar said. "But the investments and the stakes are high too."

What makes Santa Monica's law unique as well as galling to apartment owners is the Rent Control Board's considerable independence and power. The elected five-member body has the authority not only to regulate rents but to control the demolition or conversion of rental units, and regulate evictions.

Responding to charges that rent control was driving down values of apartment buildings and discouraging construction, the Rent Control Board issued a report last year saying that "rent controls appear to have no demonstrable adverse effect on newly constructed rental units . . . or on the resale value of residential rental properties."

But local realtors maintain that the regulation has had an extremely debilitating effect. Real estate values on Santa Monica apartments have remained about the same since rent control was implemented, while prices of buildings in West Los Angeles generally have doubled between 1979 and 1984, according to Albinas Markevicius, president of the Santa Monica Board of Realtors.

For example, the value of a 10-unit apartment building in Santa Monica has not risen from the $400,000 to $450,000 it was worth in 1979. During the same period, a comparable building in West Los Angeles rose in value from about $350,000 to as much as $750,000.

"We're seeing almost no sales activity," said real estate executive Fred Sands. "No one really wants to buy in Santa Monica unless they can get a steal."

Apartment owners charge that the board has set unnecessarily harsh standards. After five years, board-allowed rent hikes are about 24% behind inflation.

The average rent in Santa Monica has risen from $280 to $300 a month in 1979 to a range of $340 to $380 a month in 1984, according to several planning studies.

[B] And, unlike rent-control laws in Los Angeles and other communities, Santa Monica's law forbids landlords from raising rents when tenants move. By keeping such a tight reign on apartment owners, the Rent Control Board claims to have saved tenants more than $160 million during the last five years.

In addition, the Rent Control Board's 45-member staff has awarded individual tenants more than $650,000 in response to more than 1,700 petitions for decreased rents and 2,350 general complaints. Apartment owners have filed 768 petitions for individual rent increases. Neither party claims to know how many of those requests have been successful.

After years of frustration, however, apartment owners recently have won trial court victories removing the board's authority to award monetary damages and set its own budget—the first signs that the powerful law may be technically flawed.

The major court rulings against the board are under appeal. Meanwhile, apartment owners are developing ever-more sophisticated strategies against rent control. One of the most unusual and costly is the practice of holding units off the market. Estimates on the percentage being withheld range from 3% to 9% of the entire apartment stock.

James Baker, spokesman for a Santa Monica landlord association known as "A Committee To Insure Owners' Needs" (ACTION), said withholding apartment units is mostly a tool for large investors who can take a tax break on their buildings. One of Santa Monica's largest apartment buildings, for instance, reportedly has more than 100 vacancies. But owners of small buildings have also withheld units to protest rent control, according to Baker.

Los Angeles economist David Shulman has worked as a consultant to the Santa Monica Rent Control Board and has also performed independent housing studies. Calling Santa Monica a "fool's paradise," he predicted that apartment withholding and other backroom maneuvering would continue.

"Before rent control, landlords left nothing on the table for tenants," said Shulman, summing up the conflict. "Now the renters are leaving nothing on the table for the landlords. It's like a war."

While many people might agree with Shulman's assessment, no one is sure when the first shot was fired.

Freeway Sparked Change

For years, Santa Monica was regarded as a sleepy beachfront town—an 8.3-square-mile conservative community that cast its presidential vote for Barry Goldwater in 1964. That character began to change in 1966, when the Santa Monica Freeway linked the small community to downtown Los Angeles.

By 1970, many of the single-family homes had been replaced by apartments. Single people constituted more than half of the city's households by 1975, and by 1977 approximately 80% of the city's residents were apartment dwellers.

Despite their numbers, the tenants were not regarded as a serious political force in the city until the late 1970s, when unbridled development led to the formation of a handful of citizens coalitions.

Median rents had risen 113% between 1970 and 1978, according to the city, more than twice the average for Los Angeles and Orange counties. Between 1978 and 1979, 1,294 housing units were demolished, a 592% increase from the previous two years. Moreover, more than 500 apartment units were converted to condominiums and thousands more conversion requests received tentative approval.

"It was an emergency situation," said Rent Control Board Chairman Wayne Bauer. "A lot of people were being displaced. You had business working completely without conscience, a kind of a speculator's Disneyland."

It was against this backdrop that retirees and young activists (many of whom were affiliated with Democratic Assemblyman Tom Hayden's Campaign for Economic Democracy) came together to form Santa Monicans for Renter's Rights, the group that created the rent-control charter amendment. Called the "flip side of Proposition 13" because it capitalized on tenants' anger at not receiving benefits from tax breaks afforded their landlords, rent control won 54% of the vote on April 10, 1979, and two of its supporters won seats on the City Council.

Sharing of Power

"Santa Monica government before rent control was the domain of a very small number of people," said City Councilman Dennis Zane, an architect of the rent-control movement. "Now they had to move over and share."

The spoils of rent control were quickly absorbed by the city's renters. Thousands of Santa Monica tenants saw their rents decline substantially through rollbacks. Most were granted outright protection from eviction. As a result of these conditions, the turnover rate dropped while the demand for housing increased.

Recent studies show that Santa Monica's vacancy rate is less than 1%. While that is roughly the same as before rent control, the apartment shortage is actually more acute now, as evidenced by the long waiting lists. The situation is exacerbated by apartment units being held off the market. A 1983 survey by the Southern California Assn. of Governments forecast that Santa Monica will need an additional 2,900 units of housing by the year 1988 in order to meet its residential demands.

The first lesson prospective tenants learn about Santa Monica is that traditional rules about renting do not apply. The classified sections of local newspapers (the most common way to find apartments in most cities) offer an average of 35 listings a day, and the majority of the vacancies are registered with rental agencies that charge fees ranging from $40 to upwards of $1,000.

Apartment owner Baker said most landlords do not advertise vacancies because the demand is too great, a statement substantiated by several other apartment owners. Landlords said that the majority of the apartments are rented to people who canvass neighborhoods on foot, leaving a citywide trail of applications and resumes. Many owners trade these applications among themselves, Baker said, assuring that they get the best tenants.

[C] As a result of the high demand, apartments are rented mostly to young professionals who earn the most money and campaign the hardest to get them. Baker, who owns three apartments buildings, estimates that the average age of his tenants has declined by about 10 years while their income has more than doubled. Charles Isham, chief of staff of the Apartment Assn. of Greater Los Angeles, said the average income in his Santa Monica apartment building has jumped in five years from $20,000 a year to $50,000 a year.

"The guy who works in a gas station or a grocery store, or the woman who works in a beauty parlor is not going to get an apartment anymore," said K. B. Huff, a longtime Santa Monica landlord. "Ironically, lower-income people have been priced out of the market by rent control."

City planners noted the trend in the housing report, stating that "there has been a significant reduction in the availability of the housing stock to low- and moderate-income people. . . . It is unlikely that the private sector and government action can restore the previous economic diversity of this community in the next 10 years."

Using pre-rent control experiences as an example, rent-control supporters answer that Santa Monica's transformation to a population of elite would have occurred faster without rent control.

Councilman Zane contended that rent control has stabilized the population. Rent Board Chairman Bauer and board member David Finkel agreed, though Finkel said the prospect of more elderly or low-income people moving to Santa Monica "isn't in the cards."

Mayor Ken Edwards, a supporter of rent control, said the law cannot address that issue. "People with families couldn't get in before rent control," Edwards said. "Rent control was the result of a problem. It didn't create the problem."

Deterioration of the housing stock, a fairly common phenomenon in rent-control cities, is another concern in Santa Monica.

The city has noted that at least 6,000 apartment units need rehabilitation or replacement. Complaints filed with the city's building and safety division have risen from 62 to 130 a year since the passage of rent control and include reports of serious electrical and plumbing problems.

Some landlords still maintain their property. But the problem has become serious enough that the Rent Control Board is considering a capital improvement incentives program. Board administrator Howell Tumlin conceded that many of the city's apartments are poorly maintained. "Regular fixes aren't being made now, and my sense is that it's pretty widespread," Tumlin said.

Landlord spokesman Baker was even more blunt. "Nothing is being done," Baker said. "No carpeting, no new paint, no drapes. Owners are operating in a survival mode. That dictates that you do the minimum repairs necessary for inhabitability."

For David and Dorothy Merken, both 79, who pay $516 a month for a two-bedroom, two-bathroom apartment with a wet bar and an electric fireplace, that means that shredded curtains, peeling wallpaper and a broken shower head don't get fixed. For others it means having to replace their own water heaters, or even walls and windows.

But with some ocean-front apartments still renting for less than a tenth of what they would fetch on an open market and with homes priced beyond the average person's reach, most tenants aren't complaining. "It's a wonderful law," Dorothy Merken said. "It has stood the test of time. And with these landlords, that's quite a test."

Opposition Toughens

Baker also conceded that rent control has stood its ground against considerable opposition. But he added that recent court victories had caused "a doubling and tripling" in the determination of landlords to overturn the law.

"We've been able to bring most of the persecution and witch hunting to an end," Baker said. "But the financial picture has not changed. . . . Our rage is still there. It's just more focused, more controlled."

Santa Monica's rent-control leadership, shaken by recent court losses and concerned that the law will suffer a defeat at the higher court level, is weighing the possibility of placing a new rent-control charter amendment before the voters. In addition, they are supporting a ballot measure that would allow tenants to purchase their apartment unit under special circumstances. But protecting the present rent-control law is their biggest concern, even though they concede it is not the final answer.

"Rent control shouldn't be something you're happy with or unhappy with," Mayor Edwards said. "It's a solution, albeit temporary, to a very intolerable situation that was occurring. It's the only plan we have right now." ■

QUESTIONS

1. Use supply and demand diagrams to illustrate the situation in the rental housing market of Santa Monica.
2. Use evidence from the article to provide three specific examples of each of the following consequences of rent control:
   a. Excess demand for apartments
   b. Decrease in quantity supplied of apartments
   c. Decrease in the quality of apartments
3. Passages A and B cover supplementary rent control provisions in Santa Monica and Los Angeles, respectively:
   a. Why might the provision cited in passage A fail to be very effective?
   b. In Los Angeles, what undesirable consequence might accompany the provision cited in passage B?

4. Who do you think are the major winners from rent control in Santa Monica? The major losers?
5. What is the irony mentioned in the title and in passage C of the article, and how has rent control caused it?
6. Given the numerous problems cited in this article, why do you think rent control persists in Santa Monica?

68

This article outlines the various effects of a higher minimum wage according to "the consensus of economists." The questions emphasize the economic reasoning behind the economists' contentions, without passing judgment on whether a higher minimum wage is "good" or "bad" per se.

The Real Costs of a Higher Minimum Wage

By JOAN BERGER with SUSAN GARLAND

In downtown Boston, a sign posted outside Woolworth's advertises full- and part-time jobs with medical, dental, and life insurance—and starting pay of $4.25 an hour and up. To attract new workers in this bustling region, employers have bid entry-level wages far above the federal minimum of $3.35 an hour. For restaurants and shops in other major urban areas, the story is much the same. It's enough to make some people declare the minimum wage a relic.

But for the 5.1 million hourly workers who still earn $3.35 or less, the government-mandated minimum wage is a vital issue. It's been six years since the last increase. Now, Senator Edward M. Kennedy (D-Mass.) and Representative Augustus F. Hawkins (D–Calif.) are sponsoring a bill to boost the minimum by 15%, to $3.85, on Jan. 1, 1988, and by 10% in each of the next two years, to $4.65 by 1990. This would raise annual wage costs of U.S. business by $20 billion by 1990, according to Data Resources, Inc.

Drawing Fire

Kennedy says the proposal is the "single most important antipoverty step" before Congress. He notes that since the minimum wage was last increased in 1981, inflation has eroded its buying power by more than 20% (chart). A full-time minimum wage worker earns just under $7,000 a year—below the poverty line for a family of three. But the bill draws fire from industry, and many economists brand it inflationary and a job-killer. These critics contend that it would hurt the least-skilled job seekers and won't do much to ease poverty. One economist calls it "the most perverse legislation" imaginable. The issue pits the compassionate against the parsimonious. Does a higher minimum wage make economic sense?

Judging from the consensus of economists, the answer is a qualified "no." Although a higher minimum would not derail U.S. efforts to regain competitiveness, it would cost some low-paid workers their jobs, raise costs for many employers, and boost the inflation rate.

If passed, the measure would immediately raise the pay of 8.8% of all hourly employees. Who are these workers? Despite the hyperbolic rhetoric, most of those who earn the minimum wage are not poor. According to Census Bureau data, only one in five comes from a family living below the poverty line. The reason: Few minimum wage earners are the sole breadwinners in their families. Most are secondary earners, and nearly one-third are teenagers. Furthermore, of those who are poor, only 12% work full time year-round. For the rest, the lack of steady jobs for low-skilled workers may be more important than the pay rate.

But a hike in the minimum would affect more than just the lowest-paid workers. If the newest worker's pay is raised from $3.35 to $3.85, the person who was earning $3.90 is likely to demand an increase to stay ahead. In this way, a pay hike for the least-experienced workers tends to ripple through the wage structure.

The timing of the raise next Jan. 1 could be tricky. It would coincide with an increase in the Social Security payroll tax paid by employers and workers, to 7.51% from 7.15% this year. Wage costs are the "sleeper" in the inflation outlook, according to forecaster Donald Ratajczak of Georgia State University.

Although pessimists see a resultant jump of one percentage point in the inflation rate in 1988, most forecasters put the increase at 0.2 to 0.6 of a point. "It's not going to set off an explosion of inflation," says Nigel Gault of DRI.

[A] A larger issue than inflation, however, may be jobs. The proposed three-step increase could cost as many as 300,000 jobs, mostly among teenagers. Teenage unemployment already exceeds 15%, compared with less than 6% for the rest of the labor force. Studies show that each 10% increase in the minimum can wipe out 1% to 3% of the jobs that would normally be created for teenagers.

Darker Side

The lowest-paid workers would be most vulnerable to job cutbacks. The closer a worker's present wage is to the future higher floor, the less his job is threatened. "The employer would tighten his belt," says Finis R. Welch of the University of California at Los Angeles. "The guys who already are making $4.20 stand a good chance of keeping their jobs. The guy making $3.35 has no chance at all." Adds Clifford J. Ehrlich, manager of human resources for Marriott Corp. and the Roy Rogers restaurants owned by Marriott. "The newest, least-skilled, least-productive people will be the most expendable."

A bolstered minimum wage might have yet a darker side: It may make it easier for employers to discriminate. When wages are set by the market, employers who would limit their hiring by race or sex face a smaller, and hence more expensive, labor supply. Job bias comes at a high price. But if the government dictates an above-market wage, a surplus of workers results and the cost of discrimination declines. "That removes the economic penalty to the employer," says Lawrence H. Summers of Harvard University. "He can choose the one who's white with blond hair."

But labor officials, who are the bill's strongest supporters, dismiss such concerns. AFL–CIO chief

economist Rudolph A. Oswald believes the impact on employment would be miniscule. In his view, a higher minimum wage would be merely an "adjustment, not a raise" to restore the minimum's earning power to where it stood during much of the 1950s and 1960s. Then it amounted to about 50% of the average wage for all workers, compared with just 38% today. Says Oswald: "It's a question of justice and right for the weakest people in society."

Labor's view is supported by an economic study commissioned by Kennedy. It concludes that unemployment will rise not more than one-tenth of a point, say from 6% to 6.1%, after the full increase. Because of changing population trends, the overall impact on jobs will be "very, very small," predicts F. Gerard Adams of the University of Pennsylvania, who conducted the study.

'Baby Bust'

The youth population is shrinking rapidly, as baby boomers head toward middle age. Since 1979 the number of workers aged 16 to 19 has declined by 1.5 million. Indeed, the so-called "baby bust" is said to be causing shortages of first-time workers. That should lead some employers to pay more than the current minimum.

But this does not tell the entire story. A new Labor Dept. study has found that teenage unemployment rose two percentage points from 1979 to 1986. The figure is startling, considering that the teenage population fell 12% in that time. The jump in youth unemployment occurred among both whites and minorities. This suggests that the 1981 hike in the minimum wage may have hurt teenagers, possibly by accelerating trends toward automation and self-service.

Opponents of a higher minimum wage also worry that companies will be less eager to train workers lacking skills. Business may instead opt for experienced workers who can justify the higher wage. Companies may also become stingier with fringe benefits. This would mean "a loss of opportunity" for the hard-core unemployed, says Jacob Mincer of Columbia University.

Yet even most of those who disapprove couch their objections in fairly mild terms. No one predicts runaway inflation or ruinous unemployment. Moreover, a higher minimum would apparently leave the recent gains in U.S. competitiveness practically untouched. Why? Because 88% of the jobs affected are in service establishments, where import competition is not much of a factor.

As for the trade-off of higher earning power for fewer jobs, Hawkins, the bill's co-sponsor, asserts that those who will gain "will far outnumber" the losers. Although a shored-up minimum wage may be an inexact

The Minimum Wage Buys a Lot Less Today

Hourly Pay
In 1981 Dollars

way of alleviating poverty, Kennedy and Hawkins say that whatever gains are made will not cost the government a cent.

But Kennedy and Hawkins may be missing the economic point. A higher minimum wage will have real costs. Back in the private sector, someone will have to foot the bill. ■

QUESTIONS

1. Consider passage A:
   a. Use a supply and demand diagram for teenage workers to illustrate (1) the workers who have lost their jobs and (2) the new workers who would like to have a job but are unable to find one.
   b. According to this passage, what is the elasticity of demand for teenage workers over the wage range under consideration?
   c. Does this information about the elasticity of demand help determine the size of group 1, group 2, or both? (Refer to part **a.**)
2. In analyzing the effects of rent control laws, many economists claim that since landlords cannot adjust the price (due to the rent control law), they will often reduce the quality of the apartments instead. What, if any, similar process seems to occur with minimum wage laws? *Hint:* Is there any discussion in the article about changes in the "quality" of the jobs offered to teenagers? Explain.
3. Why do economists contend that a higher minimum wage would be more likely to hurt black teenagers than white teenagers?
4. Which groups do you think will benefit from a higher minimum wage? Which groups will be worse off?
5. Some have proposed that there be a lower minimum wage for teenagers than for adults—e.g., a "subminimum wage" for teens. How would such a "subminimum wage" for teens affect your answer to question 4?

Careful analysis, using only the basic tools of supply and demand, rejects the common assertion, appearing in this article, that government policy toward the tobacco industry is in direct conflict with the government's efforts to reduce cigarette smoking. The questions concern not only the effects of tobacco price supports and allotments but also the extent to which these policies conflict with the government's efforts to reduce smoking.

Push to Snuff Out Subsidy Lights Fears

By PAUL HOUSTON

EAST BEND, N.C.—If Congress kills the federal tobacco program, Charles Wooten says softly as he steers a pickup truck across the red clay soil of his prosperous tobacco farm, "there'll be ghost towns in this state from the mountains to the sea."

A few miles down Tobacco Road, self-styled rebel farmer Jim Canoy, head of a group pressing Congress to do away with 47 years of tobacco price supports, scoffs at such dire predictions. Canoy argues that a free market is just the tonic for an industry threatened by anti-smoking crusaders, costly stockpiles of surplus tobacco, billowing imports and wasted export opportunities.

"I'm not going to let up until it's fixed so anybody in the United States can grow tobacco if they want to," Canoy rasped. He especially objects to the federal government's production control system, under which farmers have to pay for the right to grow tobacco.

Turmoil in Industry

The diametrically opposite views of these two tobacco farmers reflect turmoil in the American tobacco industry that is unprecedented in its more than 300-year history. The tobacco industry—which dates to the days when Jamestown colonists learned from the Indians how to grow the golden leaf and thus helped finance development of the New World—today is beset by at least three major problems:

■ It has become so deeply entangled with the government that many industry leaders contend it can no longer stand on its own, especially when U.S. growers face a rising level of cheaper imported tobacco.

■ Farm subsidies in general are under assault because of soaring budget deficits, and the tobacco program costs taxpayers an estimated $100 million a year to subsidize about 200,000 tobacco growers.

■ The idea of government subsidies for tobacco has become particularly hard to defend in the face of mounting evidence of the health hazards posed by tobacco—evidence that the government itself has helped develop and disseminate.

Much at Stake

At stake in the debate over the tobacco program is not only the livelihood of the industry but also the future of smoking in the United States. Without the federal program, the price of cigarettes would probably fall, but the tobacco industry contends that the quality of its product would drop just as fast.

What is spreading alarm and controversy through the fields and curing sheds of the tobacco states—chiefly North Carolina and Kentucky—is an increasingly powerful drive in Congress to abolish the government price support program outright.

[A] Says Rep. Thomas E. Petri (R–Wis.), chief sponsor of a bill to abolish the tobacco program, "It makes no sense to warn people about the hazards of smoking on the one hand and subsidize tobacco on the other."

The drive for repeal promises to influence the struggle over all the government's farm price support programs. President Reagan is proposing to slash farm benefits across the board, and the tobacco lobby's most powerful friend in Washington—Senate Agriculture Committee Chairman Jesse Helms (R–N.C.)—is well positioned to help him if his colleagues do not support tobacco.

"Whatever farm bill comes out of the Senate will

have to have Helms' stamp of approval,'' Rep. Leon E. Panetta (D–Carmel Valley) notes. ''That's very important leverage.''

Helms and other tobacco-state lawmakers have served notice that the multibillion-dollar dairy program—which Petri would like to preserve for his Wisconsin farmers—is especially ripe for counter-attack. ''I expect maybe Mr. Petri will hear from us'' when Congress takes up the dairy program, said Rep. Larry J. Hopkins (R-Ky.), the senior Republican on the House Agriculture subcommittee on tobacco.

Under the tobacco program, the government grants ''allotments'' based on history of tobacco production. To grow tobacco, farmers must have allotments—many of which are ''leased'' each year from non-farmers who have acquired title to them over the years through inheritance of purchase.

With an allotment, a farmer is eligible for payments on tobacco at a subsidized price—currently averaging about $1.75 a pound. If the market price exceeds the subsidized price, farmers can sell their tobacco and pocket the profit. If it does not, farmers in effect sell their tobacco to the government for the subsidized price.

These days, with the dollar high and foreign tobacco prices low, the government increasingly ends up getting the tobacco.

Compromise Sought

In an effort to save the program, a leading cigarette manufacturer and key farmer groups have begun urgent negotiations on a compromise plan designed to reduce the cost to Washington. The two sides are close to a deal under which farmers would accept sharply reduced price supports, and cigarette makers in return would buy up today's massive stockpiles of tobacco and help farmers pick up future costs of lead stored by the government.

Program supporters hope that this proposition—which still has to be ratified by other cigarette companies, the Reagan Administration and possibly Congress—will deflect congressional enemies, who think they finally have the votes to repeal the price-support program this year.

Opponents forced major changes in the program in 1982 and 1983 after coming within a few votes of killing it in 1981. Tobacco farmers must now pay ''assessments'' designed to offset most of the government's cost of operating the subsidy program.

But the tobacco subsidy has shown surprising resilience, thanks largely to the political skills of tobacco-state congressmen. And Rep. Charlie Rose (D–N.C.), pointedly noting that Congress' 50-odd ''tobacco boys'' have given vital support to the pet projects of numerous colleagues, is counting on enough favors being returned to stave off repeal again this year.

''We have made a lot of friends through the years with the House leadership and with the New York City and Chrysler people'' on bailout bills, Rose said. ''I even led a group of folks to build subways for Los Angeles, so that we could be remembered in our time of trouble.

Even if Rose is correct and Congress maintains the program, it could self-destruct as a result of its own internal problems. As tobacco consumption has dropped and leaf in storage has grown, the cost of the assessments paid by farmers has risen so high that many farmers may walk away from the program.

To Petri, who is backed by a coalition of free-traders, anti-smoking advocates and some disenchanted farmers, the next logical step is to abolish the entire program. Now that the government operates the subsidy program at relatively little cost, their prime target is the allotment system that regulates who may grow tobacco, how much they may grow and what they must pay for the right to grow it.

''We have got to free our farmers to compete in the world market,'' Petri says. ''A recent study at North Carolina State University concluded that tobacco deregulation would result in a doubling of our tobacco exports, a virtual elimination of imports and an increase in the total demand for U.S. tobacco of 50% to 100% or more.''

Opponents protest that about three-fourths of allotment owners grow no tobacco at all. ''The system is feudalistic,'' Petri charged. ''Farmers' profits are soaked up by a largely absentee class of landlords who own the government-granted rights to market this crop.''

The allotment system's proponents contend that repeal would depress land values throughout the South, drive most small farmers out of business and deprive many retired farmers and widows of income derived from allotment rentals.

''If you want to cause real economic chaos in the Southeastern states,'' Hopkins said, ''I can think of no better way to do it.''

Rose, chairman of the House tobacco subcommittee, points out that Congress has already passed legislation phasing out absentee ownership of allotments by next year. But ending the allotment system altogether, he contends, would merely throw the market open to big growers.

''If you're hung up about smoking, don't punish the little grower and say you saved America from the evil weed,'' Rose said. ''The cigarette companies will laugh all the way to the bank.''

In complete agreement is Charles Wooten, a sixth-generation grower who is getting ready to plant 32 acres of tobacco seedlings on his rolling farm west of Winston-Salem.

"If you don't have some type of quota control, you could have a boom crop one year and maybe a bust for four or five years," Wooten said. Although he finds it frustrating to hunt for quota rentals each year, especially with quota sizes being cut back as stockpiles rise, he does not feel exploited.

"Most of these (allotment holders) are widows or widowers," Wooten said. "This is what they have invested in all their life to have as their retirement income."

Wooten is an unusually large tobacco grower, however. Most are small-scale operators, and Rep. Panetta says that, if the tobacco program disappeared, "these small farmers can be moved into other crops."

Rep. Hopkins rejoins: "These concrete cowboys who represent Los Angeles and New York think a Kentucky tobacco farmer sits out on the back porch with a mint julep in his hand, watching the wind blow 10,000 acres of tobacco. Well, the average size allotment is one-half acre. Try growing potatoes, corn or kumquats on that."

Both Hopkins and Rose are pressing cigarette companies to go along with the tentative agreement that has been worked out by R. J. Reynolds, the second largest manufacturer, and farmer groups in North Carolina and Kentucky. Rose has threatened to support cigarette tax hikes if No. 1 producer Philip Morris and four smaller companies balk.

Under the agreement, guaranteed minimum prices for tobacco would be slashed by about 30 cents a pound, bringing them closer to prices in Brazil, Zimbabwe and elsewhere abroad. In return, the companies would agree to spend more than $1 billion to buy up tobacco stockpiles at discounts of up to 90%. The deal would cost taxpayers about $450 million.

Economically, the cigarette companies would seem to profit greatly from lower prices that a free market would surely bring. But Reynolds spokesman David Fishel said that the companies are worried that quality would suffer if inexperienced, large-scale operators got into the act.

"Our biggest concern in keeping a Winston a Winston and a Salem a Salem," he said.

The Reagan Administration, which has proposed major price-support slashes in other farm programs, has not yet decided what to recommend for tobacco. Assistant Agriculture Secretary Wilmer (Vinegar Bend) Mizell says the Administration has two goals: to please Helms and to give the industry a chance to come up with proposed changes.

Mizell, a former congressman who represented the Winston-Salem area, suggested that the Administration would go along with the industry's tentative deal.

"If all this transpires," he said of the deal, "I think the program will be in good shape." ■

QUESTIONS

1. The Department of Agriculture's price support for tobacco keeps the price of tobacco above the market equilibrium price and also limits the amount of land that can be devoted to tobacco production. Show the effects of these policies in a supply and demand diagram for tobacco.
2. What effect does the tobacco price support program have on the price of cigarettes? What effect does the program have on the quantity of cigarettes smoked? Use a cigarette market supply and demand diagram to support your answer.
3. Consider passage A:
   a. Illustrate the effects of "warning people about the hazards of smoking" in the market for cigarettes.
   b. Is Representative Petri correct? In other words, are these two programs at odds with respect to the goal of reducing cigarette consumption? Explain carefully.

Ticket scalping has negative connotations, but the phenomenon seems quite different after considering it from an economic perspective. This article concerns the resale market for tickets to Britain's Wimbledon finals. The accompanying questions deal with excess demand, consumer surplus, opportunity cost, and the efficiency of ticket scalping.

British Officials Aren't About to Fine Ticket Scalpers for Making Huge Profit

LONDON (UPI)—British government officials have rejected a demand that penalties be placed on ticket scalpers, who are reportedly selling Wimbledon tennis championship tickets at more than 3,500% of face value.

One Conservative parliamentarian even praised the scalpers for practicing "market economics," the backbone of Prime Minister Margaret Thatcher's economic policies.

Scalpers are reportedly selling $44.25 tickets for the final match at Wimbledon for $1,590.

"If the upper-class twits who run the All-England Lawn Tennis Assn. sell their tickets at below the market prices, they can hardly grumble," said parliamentarian Theresa Gorman in a radio interview. "All the people who we insult by calling them touts are setting up a market."

Earlier, in the House of Commons, Sports Minister Colin Moynihan turned down a request from a spokesman of the Social and Liberal Democrat Party for a measure that would enable ticket scalpers to be fined up to $17,700. Moynihan said it was up to sports organizers and others, such as theater managements, to put their own house in order.

During the tournament, there have been 25 scalpers arrested in the vicinity of the Wimbledon grass courts in southwest London. Ticket scalping is not illegal, and the scalpers were charged only with obstructing the highway. Each was fined $88.50. ∎

QUESTIONS

1. Draw a demand and supply diagram for Wimbledon championship tickets and use price information from the article to
   a. Depict the "free market" price of tickets, and
   b. Depict the relationship between quantity of tickets supplied and quantity demanded at the "official" ticket price. *Hint:* Your supply curve should be vertical, since stadium capacity predetermines the number of tickets available.
2. Suppose you are a tennis fan who buys a ticket at the official price and just barely prefers attending the Wimbledon finals instead of selling your ticket at the market price. If scalping were effectively prevented anyway, how much consumer surplus would you enjoy from attending the match? Explain briefly.
3. Based on the article, how large is the opportunity cost of attending the Wimbledon finals? Explain briefly.
4. Who, if anyone, gains from ticket scalping? Who, if anyone, loses?
5. Decide whether you agree with the following statement, and briefly explain your decision: "A ban on ticket scalping increases the chance that some fans attending the Wimbledon finals will value the event less highly than other fans who end up without tickets."

Los Angeles Times, June 24, 1988. Reprinted with the permission of United Press International, copyright 1988.

This article reports the total revenue before and after the price of first-run movies at a theater complex had been increased. The questions make use of this information to calculate numerically the price elasticity of demand (over the price range under consideration) as well as the change in consumer surplus. The questions also illustrate how moviegoer comments in the article reflect basic economic concepts.

Price Hike: Coming Soon to a Theater Near You?

By ELIZABETH HAYES

Are Los Angeles moviegoers going to start thinking twice about buying movie tickets?

On Wednesday, Cineplex Odeon raised ticket prices from $6 to $6.50 in Los Angeles just as the three summer blockbusters—"Rambo III," "Crocodile Dundee II" and "Willow" began stiff competition for ticket buyers. Other chains—Pacific Theaters, AMC Entertainment, Inc. and Laemmle—are charging up to $6 but say they plan no immediate price hike.

[A] A spokesman for Cineplex Odeon said Friday that prices were raised "to maintain standards of operation. We increased prices the minimum amount we could. We've had no resistance. People want to enjoy a clean environment and will pay a premium for that luxury."

[B] However, while Tuesday's pre-hike box-office receipts at Cineplex Universal totaled $5,010 for both screens showing "Willow," on Wednesday, the first day of the increases, receipts dropped to $3,294. On Thursday, receipts rose slightly to $3,591.

Officials at Mann and Edwards theaters could not be reached for comment on possible boosts in ticket prices. (The trade paper Variety on Wednesday reported that the Mann chain was considering an increase to $7.)

"We watch what the big guys are doing," said Bob Laemmle, chief officer of Laemmle Theaters. "We're forced into following suit if the general trend goes to higher ticket prices. Cineplex Odeon started a trend in New York, so maybe they'll start one here."

Reactions of moviegoers to the price hike at Cineplex Odeon theaters—announced by the Canadian exhibition giant on Wednesday—ranged from surprise to disgust Thursday afternoon.

Some sample responses:

[C] "It's ridiculous to pay $6.50," said Judy Vaccaro of Tarzana. "That's why everybody waits until it comes out on video, so you can rent it for a buck."

"It's horrible," said Randy Davidson of Wichita, Kan., who was here on vacation. As with many visitors polled in front of the theater Thursday, he couldn't help comparing the seemingly hefty ticket price with the going rate at home—$5 tops.

"I can't believe it," said Stephanie Amato of La Canada. "This movie ["Willow"] better be good. . . . I'm going to be much more selective next time."

Not everyone was aghast, however.

"I think it's a reasonable increase," said Chris Bennington of Sherman Oaks. "I got it all out of my system when it went up to $5."

"We pay $4.50 in Washington, but if it's a really comfortable theater with 70-millimeter and Dolby, I don't mind," said Linda Nobis.

The novelty of the not-quite-year-old 18-screen multiplex continues to hold many in thrall, despite the more expensive tickets.

"The only reason I'm here is because it's a tourist attraction," said Paul Walker of Rogue River, Ore. "I'm killing two birds with one stone—seeing the new theater and the film."

"I pay it here because my car is safe here and also the size of the movie screens, the sound and atmosphere. And it's clean," said a Studio City man who called himself Ski.

At the Mann Village in Westwood, some members of the Thursday evening "Willow" crowd called the going rate there of $6 "outrageous."

"It's too high. I get [a discount on] tickets from school. Otherwise, I wouldn't come at all," said UCLA student Nancy Schmidt.

[D] Steve Curtis, a student at Cal State North-

ridge, said that if ticket prices go up at Mann Village he will go across the street to the Bruin and pay $6, regardless of the films being screened.

"It's kind of like what's happening to postage stamps," said Melinda MacInnis of Long Beach. "[Six dollars] is a lot of money."

When ticket prices soared to $7 at 44 Manhattan movie theaters last December, moviegoers were blase. But New York Mayor Edward I. Koch ran a crusade to boycott theaters on Monday nights. He stationed himself in front of the Baronet and Coronet Theaters in midtown Manhattan, while patrons strolled past him to see "Broadcast News."

After 46 days, in late February, Koch gave up his boycott campaign due to lack of interest from the public.

In Los Angeles, Mayor Tom Bradley's press secretary said the mayor would not comment on the new prices. ■

QUESTIONS

1. Consider passage B:
   a. Use the information from Tuesday's and Wednesday's receipts to complete the missing items in the table below about the demand for "Willow" over the $6.00 to $6.50 range. Explain your calculations.

Price	Number of Tickets Sold
$6.00	
$6.50	

   b. Now use the information in the table to compute the price elasticity of demand over this price range.
2. a. Define consumer surplus.
   b. Based on the information in the table above, diagram the demand curve for "Willow" and indicate on your diagram the change in consumer surplus that resulted on Wednesday from the price increasing from $6.00 to $6.50.
   c. Calculate a numerical value for this change in consumer surplus. (For the purposes of this question, assume that the demand curve is a straight line.)
3. Consider passage A: Is this statement by the spokesman for Cineplex consistent with your answer to question 1? Explain your answer.
4. Consider passages C and D:
   a. What would these comments alone (without any other information) lead you to conclude about the elasticity of demand for movies in the price range of $6.00 to $6.50?
   b. Play the pretentious economist and summarize by completing the missing words in the following statement: "The easier it is to find ——, the —— (larger, smaller) the price elasticity of demand for movie-going."

This is a more difficult article on elasticity of demand. New York City's Taxi and Limousine Commission and the Metropolitan Taxicab Board of Trade use conflicting elasticity assumptions to predict the consequences of a taxi fare increase. The two estimates raise a number of questions about the relationship between total revenue changes and elasticity of demand.

Despite Fare Rise, Taxi Fleets Report New Losses Again

The city's taxi fleets have found the fare increase granted last fall inadequate and are preparing to seek a new increase, according to Taxi News, the industry's paper.

The 17.5 percent fare increase that went into effect in November has produced only about a 10 to 11 percent increase in gross revenues rather than the 17.5 percent that the Taxi and Limousine Commission had predicted, the paper said. As a result, the paper said, the possibility of operational profit has been wiped out and losses are building up again, because "operating costs have continued to inflate."

[A] The industry's paper said that the Metropolitan Taxicab Board of Trade, representing the city's 60 fleet owners would probably demand that the Taxi Commission "live up to its commitment to give them the fare increase that will provide the 17.5 percent increase in gross revenue.

"According to industry accountants, that can only be done by reshaping the fare upward to the 25 percent schedule they originally submitted," the paper added.

The Taxi News also suggested that the industry was expected to put forward a plan to offset the rising costs of gasoline. This might take the form of charging passengers 1 cent for each 2 cents per gallon of increased gasoline costs, the paper said. If gasoline costs dropped, it said, the procedure would be reversed, and 1 cent would be taken off the trip cost for each 2-cent reduction in the cost of gasoline.

The Metropolitan Taxicab Board of Trade has called a news conference for this morning to announce details of its plans and to document the fleet industry's needs, a spokesman said. ■

QUESTIONS

1. Given that the 17.5 percent fare increase that went into effect has produced only about a 10 to 11 percent increase in gross revenues, is the demand for taxis elastic or inelastic over the price range under consideration in this article? Explain briefly.
2. The Taxi and Limousine Commission had *predicted* that the 17.5 percent fare increase would increase gross revenues by 17.5 percent. What does such a prediction imply about the commission's view of the numerical value of the price elasticity of demand for taxis?
3. Consider passage A: Based on this passage, which group has assumed the greater elasticity of demand for taxis, the industry accountants representing the Metropolitan Taxicab Board of Trade, or the Taxi and Limousine Commission? Explain your reasoning.

For classes that cover the incidence of a per unit tax, this article can reinforce that lesson by illustrating how incidence can be misunderstood in practice. The article traces court efforts to determine who really paid a 20 percent tax on X-rated movies.

X-FLIX TAX

The X-FLIX TAX came from box-office bux, South Carolina's top court says.

In 1984, the state Supreme Court declared that South Carolina's 20% admissions tax on X-rated and unrated movies was unconstitutional. Multi-Cinema Ltd., a theater chain, sought a refund, which was denied by the state tax commission. The state said that tax was paid by theater-goers and only they could seek refunds. The theater chain appealed to a court and won, so the state appealed to the state Supreme Court.

The Supreme Court said the state law imposing a general tax on movie admissions specifies that it shall be paid by the person paying for admission. Yet the overturned law providing for "a license tax . . . on admissions" to X-rated films contained no such language. Because that specific provision was missing, Chief Judge Ness and two other judges concluded that legislators meant the tax to be paid by theaters. They upheld a refund to Multi-Cinema.

But dissenting Judge Gregory said that "perverts" legislative intent. ∎

QUESTIONS

1. Since the 20 percent X-rated movie tax was declared unconstitutional, a refund was due to those who had paid the tax. The courts are trying to determine who the legislators meant to pay the tax.
   a. Would an economist think that the legislators' intent was relevant to who really ends up paying the tax? Explain carefully.
   b. What is wrong with just having the court look up who actually sent the tax payments to the South Carolina State Treasury in determining who actually paid them?

2. Show the effect of the 20 percent tax on a supply and demand diagram, and then explain, according to your diagram, how much of the tax is really paid by theater owners.

3. Under what supply and/or demand conditions would it make economic sense to claim that the theater owners paid the full amount of the tax?

This selection consists of Major League baseball batting averages reported over two consecutive weeks. An attractive feature of batting averages is the easy availability of averages that move in different ways. The behavior of batting averages helps illustrate how marginal and average values are related.

Major League Batting Averages

Averages for two consecutive weeks appear on page 44. Note: To compute a batting average for any time period, divide total hits by total at bats for that time period.

QUESTIONS

1. The tables here contain Major League baseball batting averages, reported on consecutive Sundays (August 7 and August 14, 1988). Use the tables to find one player whose batting average fell during the week and another whose average rose. Then, for each player, complete a table similar to the one below.

	At Bats	Hits	Batting Average
Name of player:			
Starting average: 8/7/88:			
Ending average: 8/14/88:			
Marginal performance: 8/7–8/14:			

2. Based on your computations from question 1, summarize how marginal values affect the behavior of average values.

3. Use the information below to compute the missing batting average information for the San Diego Padres' Tony Gwynn:

	At Bats	Hits	Batting Average
Starting average: 8/7/88:	343	105	.306
Ending average 1: 8/14/88:	371	117	.315
Marginal performance 1: 8/7–8/14:			
Ending average 2: 8/21/88:	395	127	.322
Marginal performance 2: 8/14–8/21:			

Given how Gwynn's marginal performance changed during the second week, why does the upward trend in Gwynn's batting average still make sense?

August 7, 1988

MAJOR LEAGUE AVERAGES

Complete through games of Friday

AMERICAN LEAGUE

TEAM BATTING

	AB	R	H	HR	RBI	Pct
Boston	3737	556	1086	81	517	.291
Minnesota ..	3713	520	1036	112	487	.279
New York ...	3669	543	997	95	502	.272
Toronto	3783	528	1011	114	494	.267
Kansas City ..	3700	470	979	85	450	.265
California ...	3753	506	992	85	466	.264
Cleveland ...	3715	480	973	96	452	.262
Detroit	3614	500	936	95	457	.259
Oakland	3833	526	983	106	494	.256
Seattle	3665	437	937	103	406	.256
Milwaukee ..	3709	441	945	73	405	.255
Texas	3593	408	911	77	379	.254
Chicago	3692	445	896	100	406	.243
Baltimore ...	3572	372	829	100	349	.232

INDIVIDUAL BATTING

270 or more at bats

	AB	R	H	HR	RBI	Pct
Puckett Min ..	445	69	159	16	83	.357
Boggs Bsn	397	82	141	4	42	.355
Winfield NY ..	371	70	125	20	78	.337
Brett KC	402	56	135	18	80	.336
Greenwell Bsn	388	58	129	18	88	.332
Mattingly NY .	370	65	121	10	59	.327
Washgtn NY ..	286	40	93	5	40	.325
Molitor Mil ...	407	74	131	7	35	.322
Hendson NY ..	339	78	109	6	33	.322
Trammll Det ..	336	54	108	11	53	.321
Burks Bsn	355	65	112	13	62	.315
Franco Cle ...	426	66	134	9	41	.315
Evans Bsn	389	63	122	10	74	.314
Seitzer KC ...	401	64	124	5	43	.309
Gaetti Min ...	401	57	121	25	71	.302
Yount Mil	420	65	127	9	57	.302
Joyner Cal ...	407	56	122	8	61	.300
Hall Cle	354	48	106	4	46	.299
Hndson Oak ..	323	63	95	16	62	.294
Lansford Oak .	428	61	126	6	44	.294
Hrbek Min	365	55	107	18	52	.293
McGriff Tor ..	349	71	102	26	63	.292
Barrett Bsn ...	429	61	125	1	47	.291
O'Brien Tex ..	371	35	108	10	42	.291
Reynolds Sea .	398	37	116	2	25	.291
Ray Cal	404	59	117	3	52	.290
Davis Cal	410	58	118	17	72	.288
Gruber Tor ...	403	56	116	13	62	.288
Larkin Min ...	356	38	102	4	49	.287
Canseco Oak .	423	87	120	31	87	.284
Davis Sea	307	43	87	13	44	.283
Salazar Det ...	321	50	91	11	49	.283
Fernndz Tor ..	433	51	122	4	43	.282
Gantner Mil ..	367	42	103	0	31	.281
Carter Cle	425	68	119	20	75	.280
Fletcher Tex ..	390	44	109	0	35	.279
CRipken Blt ...	381	61	106	18	61	.278
Javier Oak ...	324	41	90	2	30	.278
Lemon Det ...	346	44	95	8	38	.275
Brookens Det .	281	48	77	5	33	.274
Snyder Cle ...	376	55	103	20	60	.274
Bell Tor	406	56	111	16	63	.273
Rice Bsn	356	41	97	8	49	.272
Baines Chi ...	402	42	109	11	48	.271
Wilson KC ...	429	53	116	1	29	.270
Guillen Chi ...	391	38	105	0	30	.269
Cotto Sea	295	38	79	5	26	.268
Tabler KC	291	33	78	1	39	.268
Trtabll KC	349	51	93	16	58	.266
Whitaker Det .	319	42	85	8	43	.266
Brantley Sea ..	383	54	101	14	44	.264
Buechle Tex ..	329	48	87	12	37	.264
Gladden Min ..	394	67	104	6	43	.264
Lyons Chi	292	33	77	5	32	.264
White Cal	313	55	82	9	36	.262
White KC	359	37	94	7	44	.262
Braggs Mil ...	272	30	71	10	42	.261
Howell Cal ...	335	39	87	10	49	.260
Incvglia Tex ..	339	49	88	20	46	.260
Murray Blt ...	407	49	106	19	53	.260
Quinones Sea .	338	40	88	8	28	.260
Jackson KC ..	279	40	72	16	47	.258
Downing Cal ..	311	61	80	17	44	.257
Stllwll KC	367	50	94	9	42	.256
Jacoby Cle ...	396	47	101	7	34	.255
Gagne Min ...	322	51	81	12	36	.252
Clark NY	338	63	85	20	70	.251
Surhoff Mil ...	336	31	84	3	21	.250
Upshaw Cle ..	359	48	89	9	38	.248
Walker Chi ...	377	45	93	8	42	.247
Weiss Oak ...	305	30	74	3	28	.243
Schofield Cal .	359	43	87	5	25	.242
Allanson Cle ..	270	24	65	4	34	.241
Santana NY ..	310	37	74	4	28	.239
McGwire Oak .	399	57	95	19	61	.238
Sierra Tex	397	49	94	15	59	.237
Pasqua Chi ...	297	38	70	15	39	.236
Moseby Tor ..	343	61	80	9	35	.233
Randolph NY .	288	33	67	1	24	.233
Sveum Mil ...	364	31	84	9	40	.231
Sheets Blt	348	28	80	7	35	.230
Pglrulo NY ...	311	33	70	9	53	.225
Barfield Tor ..	285	36	62	10	33	.218
Deer Mil	306	40	66	12	44	.216
Pettis Det	368	54	79	3	34	.215
Presley Sea ...	375	34	80	12	42	.213
Evans Det	297	31	61	14	40	.205
Parrish Bsn ...	292	26	58	9	35	.199
BRipken Blt ...	363	39	72	1	23	.198

NATIONAL LEAGUE

TEAM BATTING

	AB	R	H	HR	RBI	Pct
Chicago	3760	420	981	75	395	.261
Los Angeles .	3678	455	945	70	429	.257
New York ...	3656	459	934	97	434	.255
Houston	3692	464	930	68	427	.252
San Francisco	3630	468	915	82	441	.252
Atlanta	3690	406	928	70	383	.251
Montreal ...	3710	418	928	71	379	.250
Pittsburgh ...	3636	452	904	83	431	.249
StLouis	3745	387	926	48	360	.247
San Diego ...	3557	375	867	57	357	.244
Cincinnati ...	3678	433	894	89	396	.243
Philadelphia .	3644	414	867	71	393	.238

INDIVIDUAL BATTING

270 or more at bats

	AB	R	H	HR	RBI	Pct
Perry Atl	358	45	115	6	53	.321
Dawson Chi ..	409	52	128	17	58	.313
Galarraga Mon	423	72	132	22	63	.312
Gibson LA ...	391	76	120	21	59	.307
Palmeiro Chi ..	420	52	129	6	30	.307
Gwynn SD ...	343	43	105	6	43	.306
Dykstra NY ...	316	47	96	3	15	.304
McGee StL ...	448	59	136	2	41	.304
Grace Chi	286	36	86	5	31	.301
Sax LA	435	54	130	5	41	.299
Bonds Pit	381	75	112	18	38	.294
Law Chi	377	45	111	8	51	.294
Thopson SF ..	337	49	99	4	35	.294
VanSlyke Pit ..	414	73	121	19	73	.292
Larkin Cin	393	63	114	10	38	.290
Bonilla Pit	398	64	115	18	66	.289
Strawbry NY ..	371	76	107	29	74	.288
McReylds NY .	380	52	109	16	63	.287
Oquendo StL .	283	15	81	3	27	.286
Butler SF	391	80	111	4	34	.284
Clark SF	388	70	110	23	85	.284
Doran Htn	336	52	95	7	49	.283
Shelby LA	318	47	90	5	41	.283
Thmpsn Phi ..	291	44	82	2	25	.282
Oberkfell Atl ..	358	35	101	3	32	.282
Bream Pit	306	35	86	8	42	.281
Raines Mon ..	344	53	96	9	37	.279
Daniels Cin ...	334	60	93	10	41	.278
Sabo Cin	388	51	108	11	42	.278
Hatcher Htn ..	389	61	107	3	35	.275
Moreland SD .	353	29	97	3	45	.275
Davis Cin	325	60	89	20	58	.274
Scioscia LA ..	277	22	76	2	27	.274
James Atl	286	35	78	2	25	.273
Brooks Mon ..	412	42	112	13	65	.272
Hayes Phi	313	36	85	5	39	.272
Davis Htn	361	57	98	22	76	.271
Smith StL	404	62	108	3	32	.267
Bass Htn	365	42	97	10	49	.266
Brunansky StL	338	49	90	15	61	.266
Mldndo SF ...	369	39	98	7	49	.266
Dunston Chi ..	408	47	108	8	47	.265
Coleman StL ..	444	57	116	2	22	.261
Marshall LA ..	415	50	108	14	61	.260
Young Htn ...	375	61	97	0	25	.259
Gant Atl	371	57	96	12	44	.259
Thomas Atl ...	432	44	112	12	54	.259
Samuel Phi ...	430	53	111	10	51	.258
Ramirez Htn ..	369	36	95	4	41	.257
Wallach Mon .	408	39	105	8	43	.257
O'Neill Cin ...	324	40	83	10	44	.256
Webster Chi ..	339	42	86	2	17	.254
Uribe SF	314	35	79	2	17	.252
Carter NY	323	26	81	8	35	.251
Sandberg Chi .	402	49	101	11	43	.251
Pena StL	360	36	90	8	36	.250
Schmidt Phi ..	369	47	91	11	61	.247
Santiago SD ..	333	33	82	4	22	.246
Lind Pit	436	55	107	2	36	.245
James Phi	378	39	91	14	45	.241
Bradley Phi ...	366	50	88	5	32	.240
DaMrtinez Mon	289	32	69	4	37	.239
Mitchell SF ...	355	44	85	16	61	.239
Alomar SD ...	343	43	82	6	23	.239
Murphy Atl ...	402	61	93	19	51	.231
Parrish Phi ...	282	32	64	12	49	.227
Johnsn NY ...	349	56	79	18	49	.226
Elster NY	299	27	65	7	30	.217
Rivera Mon ...	287	26	62	4	25	.216

August 14, 1988

MAJOR LEAGUE AVERAGES

Complete through games of Friday

AMERICAN LEAGUE

TEAM BATTING

	AB	R	H	HR	RBI	Pct
Boston	3973	580	1146	84	541	.288
Minnesota ..	3915	549	1096	120	514	.280
New York ...	3870	567	1047	103	525	.271
Toronto	4028	555	1074	121	520	.267
Kansas City ..	3946	504	1047	93	482	.265
Cleveland ...	3951	504	1037	101	474	.262
California ...	3972	524	1036	89	483	.261
Oakland	4063	568	1053	112	533	.259
Detroit	3802	515	975	96	471	.256
Seattle	3892	467	992	109	432	.255
Milwaukee ..	3935	474	994	80	437	.253
Texas	3827	430	966	79	395	.252
Chicago	3938	474	961	106	432	.244
Baltimore ...	3790	396	884	105	373	.233

INDIVIDUAL BATTING

286 or more at bats

	AB	R	H	HR	RBI	Pct
Boggs Bsn ...	426	83	152	4	44	.357
Puckett Min ..	468	75	166	17	85	.355
Greenwell Bsn	415	61	138	18	90	.333
Hendson NY ..	357	82	117	6	36	.328
Washgtn NY ..	305	43	100	6	44	.328
Brett KC	428	59	140	19	83	.327
Mattingly NY .	394	70	129	11	64	.327
Winfield NY ..	394	71	128	20	78	.325
Molitor Mil ...	431	79	139	9	42	.323
Trammll Det ..	356	57	114	11	55	.320
Franco Cle ...	452	68	143	10	44	.316
Burks Bsn	381	68	118	13	63	.310
Seitzer KC ...	418	66	129	5	46	.309
Hedson Oak ..	352	69	107	17	68	.304
Evans Bsn	414	67	125	10	75	.302
Hrbek Min	386	59	115	21	58	.298
Yount Mil	449	68	134	9	63	.298
Gaetti Min ...	424	61	126	26	75	.297
McGriff Tor ..	372	75	109	27	65	.293
Hall Cle	380	50	111	4	48	.292
Lansford Oak .	452	64	132	6	50	.292
Ray Cal	428	61	124	4	58	.290
Reynolds Sea .	425	39	123	2	25	.289
Joyner Cal ...	431	56	124	8	61	.288
Davis Sea	327	48	94	15	48	.287
Canseco Oak .	450	90	129	31	91	.287
Larkin Min ...	376	41	108	5	52	.287
Gruber Tor ...	427	58	122	13	63	.286
O'Brien Tex ..	397	36	113	10	46	.285
Davis Cal	436	59	124	17	73	.284
Fernndz Tor ..	461	53	131	4	48	.284
Salazar Det ...	339	51	96	11	52	.283
Gantner Mil ..	388	45	109	0	32	.281
Rice Bsn	378	43	106	9	53	.280
Barrett Bsn ...	451	61	126	1	47	.279
Gladden Min ..	417	72	115	7	45	.276
Snyder Cle ...	391	57	108	20	62	.276
Baines Chi ...	429	44	118	12	56	.275
Fletcher Tex ..	414	45	114	0	37	.275
Tabler KC	316	36	87	1	44	.275
Javier Oak ...	332	42	91	2	30	.274
Brookens Det .	297	48	81	5	34	.273
Guillen Chi ...	417	41	114	0	30	.273
CRipken Blt ...	405	67	110	20	64	.272
Lemon Det ...	367	45	100	8	38	.272
WWilson KC ..	449	56	122	1	30	.272
Carter Cle	454	70	123	20	75	.271
Bell Tor	432	56	116	16	65	.269
Murray Blt ...	433	54	116	21	60	.268
Lyons Chi	319	38	85	5	32	.266
Quinones Sea .	357	45	95	8	31	.266
White Cal	341	58	90	9	39	.264
White KC	382	41	101	8	45	.264
Stllwll KC	397	56	105	10	46	.264
Cotto Sea	315	40	83	5	27	.263
Whitaker Det .	327	45	86	8	43	.263
Brantley Sea ..	407	57	106	14	46	.260
Incvglia Tex ..	363	52	94	21	49	.259
Trtabll KC	374	57	97	18	63	.259
Gagne Min ...	340	53	87	12	39	.256
Jackson KC ..	306	42	78	17	50	.255
Howell Cal ...	355	43	90	11	51	.254
Buechle Tex ..	350	50	88	12	38	.251
McGwire Oak .	423	63	106	21	70	.251
Upshaw Cle ..	383	49	96	10	43	.251
Jacoby Cle ...	420	51	105	8	36	.250
Downing Cal ..	333	62	83	18	45	.249
Clark NY	355	66	88	22	73	.248
Walker Chi ...	377	45	93	8	42	.247
Santana NY ..	332	38	81	4	28	.244
Surhoff Mil ...	355	32	86	3	23	.242
Allanson Cle ..	290	25	69	4	34	.238
Weiss Oak ...	320	31	76	3	28	.238
Schofield Cal .	379	45	90	5	26	.237
Pasqua Chi ...	320	40	75	16	42	.234
Moseby Tor ..	343	61	80	9	35	.233
Randolph NY .	288	33	67	1	24	.233
Sierra Tex	424	53	99	16	61	.233
Deer Mil	330	43	76	14	50	.230
Sheets Blt	364	29	83	7	35	.228
Sveum Mil ...	381	34	87	9	41	.228
Pglrulo NY ...	318	33	70	9	53	.220
Barfield Tor ..	310	40	68	11	35	.219
Presley Sea ...	398	36	86	13	46	.216
Pettis Det	368	54	79	3	34	.215
Evans Det	305	32	63	14	42	.207
BRipken Blt ...	383	42	77	1	24	.201
Parrish Bsn ...	295	26	59	9	36	.200

NATIONAL LEAGUE

TEAM BATTING

	AB	R	H	HR	RBI	Pct
Chicago	3962	449	1038	77	420	.262
Los Angeles .	3923	485	1010	75	456	.257
San Francisco	3881	505	985	87	474	.254
New York ...	3905	490	991	104	462	.254
Montreal ...	3957	455	998	78	413	252
Atlanta	3946	435	990	77	411	251
Houston	3906	487	977	69	447	250
Pittsburgh ...	3909	483	976	85	457	250
StLouis	3980	412	985	51	385	.247
Cincinnati ...	3885	462	950	97	423	245
San Diego ...	3782	397	921	62	378	244
Philadelphia .	3874	444	929	77	423	240

INDIVIDUAL BATTING

286 or more at bats

	AB	R	H	HR	RBI	Pct
Perry Atl	388	48	124	6	56	320
Gwynn SD ...	371	46	117	6	47	315
Dawson Chi ..	433	57	136	17	60	314
Galarraga Mon	453	74	140	22	64	309
Palmeiro Chi ..	440	56	136	6	35	309
Grace Chi	309	40	95	5	33	307
Gibson LA ...	419	83	127	22	63	303
Dykstra NY ...	347	50	103	5	22	297
Sax LA	462	56	137	5	43	297
Law Chi	399	47	118	8	56	296
McGee StL ...	476	60	140	2	44	294
Bonilla Pit	426	72	125	19	73	293
Bream Pit	338	38	99	8	51	293
VanSlyke Pit ..	441	80	129	19	74	293
Bonds Pit	416	78	121	19	42	291
Thopson SF ..	362	51	105	4	36	290
Larkin Cin	419	66	121	10	42	289
McReylds NY .	405	56	117	17	70	289
Butler SF	416	85	120	4	35	288
Thmpsn Phi ..	309	46	88	2	20	285
Clark SF	414	76	117	24	87	283
Sabo Cin	414	56	117	11	42	283
Oberkfell Atl ..	379	37	107	3	33	282
Brooks Mon ..	438	47	123	15	68	281
Daniels Cin ...	349	64	98	12	43	281
Oquendo StL .	308	16	86	3	29	279
James Atl	307	38	85	3	27	277
Doran Htn	358	56	99	7	50	277
Davis Cin	347	63	96	20	61	277
Scioscia LA ..	300	25	83	2	31	277
Hatcher Htn ..	406	63	112	3	38	276
Raines Mon ..	370	58	102	10	42	276
Davis Htn	386	59	106	22	78	275
Marshall LA ..	444	54	121	17	67	273
Strawbry NY ..	396	77	108	29	76	273
Hayes Phi	313	36	85	5	39	272
Shelby LA	343	48	93	5	43	271
Moreland SD .	374	29	101	3	48	270
Smith StL	429	64	116	3	35	270
O'Neill Cin ...	346	46	93	13	50	269
Bass Htn	389	45	104	11	57	267
Coleman StL ..	474	60	126	3	26	266
Dunston Chi ..	423	52	112	8	47	265
Brunansky StL	364	51	96	16	63	264
Gant Atl	398	65	105	14	48	264
Mldndo SF ...	386	40	101	7	51	262
Thomas Atl ...	463	44	120	12	56	259
Wallach Mon .	433	42	112	10	48	259
Ramirez Htn ..	392	37	101	4	43	258
Sandberg Chi .	427	52	109	11	45	255
Samuel Phi ...	456	55	116	10	55	254
Mitchell SF ...	380	49	96	18	67	253
Pena StL	376	41	95	8	36	253
Young Htn ...	393	62	99	0	26	252
Bradley Phi ...	394	53	98	6	35	249
Carter NY	343	29	85	9	37	248
Schmidt Phi ..	391	52	97	12	62	248
Webster Chi ..	363	45	90	3	19	248
Uribe SF	340	37	84	2	22	247
Santiago SD ..	357	38	88	7	28	246
Alomar SD ...	365	46	89	7	26	244
James Phi	401	43	97	15	49	242
Lind Pit	466	60	112	2	36	240
DaMrtinez Mon	301	33	72	4	38	239
Murphy Atl ...	430	66	101	22	62	235
Parrish Phi ...	298	34	69	13	54	232
Rivera Mon ...	295	29	67	4	26	227
Elster NY	316	31	71	7	31	225
Johnsn NY ...	374	61	84	20	51	225

U.S. income taxes are useful for improving the understanding of marginal values and the relationship between marginal and average values. In this selection, 1987 federal income tax tables provide information for computing total taxes, and average and marginal tax rates. The last question deals with a"letter to the editor" in which the letter writer makes the common mistake of claiming that total taxes rise by more than income when a taxpayer moves into a higher tax bracket.

1987 Tax Rate Schedules

Schedules X, Y, Z appear on page 46.

QUESTIONS

1. Use Schedule X for single taxpayers to complete an income tax table similar to the one below:

Taxable Income*	Income Tax	Average Tax (as a Percentage of Taxable Income)	Marginal Tax Rate
$ 5,000			
25,000			
45,000			
65,000			
85,000			

*"Taxable income" corresponds to the Schedule X label, "amount on form 1040, line 36"

2. What happens to an individual's average tax rate as income rises? Why?
3. Consider the following excerpts from a letter to the editor of the *Los Angeles Times:*

> Taxpayers with a taxable income at the borderline between . . . two brackets . . . need an extraordinary raise in salary (or other income) to maintain the spendable income available in the lower bracket.

For example a couple filing a joint return with a taxable income of $27,500 would be taxed at the rate of 15%. Their income tax would be $4,125, thereby leaving them with $23,375 in spendable after-tax dollars.

Now assume the couple receives a 5% salary increase ($1,375 a year) which raises their taxable income to $28,875 and puts the couple in the 28% tax bracket. The couple would now pay $8,085 in taxes, which would leave them $20,790 in after-tax dollars.

Therefore the couple would have been better off to refuse the salary increase.

a. Does this letter writer think "tax bracket" refers to the marginal or the average tax rate? Support your answer.
b. How large would the value of a marginal tax rate have to be for the couple to really be "better off to refuse the salary increase"?
c. Without using technical language, provide a brief (one- or two-sentence) "editor's response" to this letter writer, clearing up any apparent confusion.

1987 Tax Rate Schedules

Caution: You may use these schedules **ONLY** if your taxable income (Form 1040, line 36) is $50,000 or more.
Example: Mr. Jones is single. His taxable income on Form 1040, line 36, is $53,525. First, he finds the schedule (Schedule X) for single taxpayers. Next, he finds the $27,000–54,000 income line. Then, he subtracts $27,000 from $53,525 and multiplies the result ($26,525) by 35%. He then adds $9,283.75 ($26,525 × .35) to $5,304 and enters the result ($14,587.75) on Form 1040, line 37.

Schedule X—Single Taxpayers

Use this schedule if you checked **Filing Status Box 1** on Form 1040—

If the amount on Form 1040, line 36 is: Over—	But not over—	Enter on Form 1040, line 37	of the amount over—
$0	$1,800	.......11%	$0
1,800	16,800	$198 + 15%	1,800
16,800	27,000	2,448 + 28%	16,800
27,000	54,000	5,304 + 35%	27,000
54,000	- - - - - - -	14,754 + 38.5%	54,000

Schedule Z—Heads of Household

(including certain married persons who live apart—see page 7 of the Instructions)

Use this schedule if you checked **Filing Status Box 4** on Form 1040—

If the amount on Form 1040, line 36 is: Over—	But not over—	Enter on Form 1040, line 37	of the amount over—
$0	$2,500	.......11%	$0
2,500	23,000	$275 + 15%	2,500
23,000	38,000	3,350 + 28%	23,000
38,000	80,000	7,550 + 35%	38,000
80,000	- - - - - - -	22,250 + 38.5%	80,000

Schedule Y—Married Taxpayers and Qualifying Widows and Widowers

Married Filing Joint Returns and Qualifying Widows and Widowers

Use this schedule if you checked **Filing Status Box 2 or 5** on Form 1040—

If the amount on Form 1040, line 36 is: Over—	But not over—	Enter on Form 1040, line 37	of the amount over—
$0	$3,000	.......11%	$0
3,000	28,000	$330 + 15%	3,000
28,000	45,000	4,080 + 28%	28,000
45,000	90,000	8,840 + 35%	45,000
90,000	- - - - - - -	24,590 + 38.5%	90,000

Married Filing Separate Returns

Use this schedule if you checked **Filing Status Box 3** on Form 1040—

If the amount on Form 1040, line 36 is: Over—	But not over—	Enter on Form 1040, line 37	of the amount over—
$0	$1,500	.......11%	$0
1,500	14,000	$165 + 15%	1,500
14,000	22,500	2,040 + 28%	14,000
22,500	45,000	4,420 + 35%	22,500
45,000	- - - - - - -	12,295 + 38.5%	45,000

This article reports the driving expenses compiled annually by Hertz Corp. The information is useful for computing and graphing average and marginal driving costs, and for determining the roles of variable costs and fixed costs for decision-making purposes.

Hertz Corp. Study

DETROIT (UPI)—For only the second time in history, the per-mile cost of owning and operating a typical new compact car dropped in 1983 by 1.4 cents to 43.28 cents, an annual Hertz Corp. study showed Sunday.

The 43.28 cents per mile driving cost was calculated based on a compact domestic sedan, such as the Ford Fairmont, driven 10,000 miles a year for five years.

The figure included fixed costs comprised of depreciation, 13.71 cents; insurance and license fees, 9.98 cents and interest, 7.66 cents. Variable costs included maintenance and repairs, 3.55 cents, and gasoline, 8.38 cents. ■

QUESTIONS

For the following questions, accept Hertz's classification of costs, and assume that variable costs remain at the same level per mile regardless of the number of miles driven.

1. Based on the Hertz Corp. estimates, how large are the *total* fixed costs of owning a Ford Fairmont?
2. Compute average fixed cost, average variable cost, average total cost, and marginal cost per mile driven for Ford Fairmont owners who drive the following number of miles per year: (a) 5,000, (b) 10,000, (c) 15,000.
3. Construct a diagram with curves showing average cost, average variable cost, and marginal cost per mile driven for a Ford Fairmont.
4. Suppose you own a Ford Fairmont and currently drive 10,000 miles per year. If your employer offers you the chance to do some on-the-job driving at a reimbursement rate of 20 cents per mile, would you volunteer? Why or why not?

This article reports on how a Continental Airlines economist uses such theoretical concepts as fixed cost, variable cost, marginal cost, and average cost to decide which flights his firm should undertake in order to maximize profits. Although a bit outdated, the article is a classic for this portion of the microeconomic principles course.

Airline Takes the Marginal Route

Continental Air Lines, Inc., last year filled only half the available seats on its Boeing 707 jet flights, a record some 15 percentage points worse than the national average.

By eliminating just a few runs—less than 5%—Continental could have raised its average load considerably. Some of its flights frequently carry as few as 30 passengers on the 120-seat plane. But the improved load factor would have meant reduced profits.

For Continental bolsters its corporate profits by deliberately running extra flights that aren't expected to do more than return their out-of-pocket costs—plus a little profit. Such marginal flights are an integral part of the over-all operating philosophy that has brought small, Denver-based Continental—tenth among the 11 trunk carriers—through the bumpy postwar period with only one loss year.

Chief Contribution

This philosophy leans heavily on marginal analysis. And the line leans heavily on Chris F. Whelan, vice-president in charge of economic planning, to translate marginalism into hard, dollars-and-cents decisions [see box].

Getting management to accept and apply the marginal concept probably is the chief contribution any economist can make to his company. Put most simply, marginalists maintain that a company should undertake any activity that adds more to revenues than it does to costs—and not limit itself to those activities whose returns equal average or "fully allocated" costs.

The approach, of course, can be applied to virtually any business, not just to air transportation. It can be used in consumer finance, for instance, where the question may be whether to make more loans—includ-

ing more bad loans—if this will increase net profit. Similarly, in advertising, the decision may rest on how much extra business a dollar's worth of additional advertising will bring in, rather than pegging the advertising budget to a percentage of sales—and, in insurance, where setting high interest rates to discourage policy loans may actually damage profits by causing policyholders to borrow elsewhere.

Communication

Whelan finds all such cases wholly analogous to his run of problems, where he seeks to keep his company's eye trained on the big objective: net profit.

He is a genially gruff, shirt-sleeves kind of airline veteran, who resembles more a sales-manager type than an economist. This facet of his personality helps him "sell" ideas internally that might otherwise be brushed off as merely theoretical or too abstruse.

Last summer, Whelan politely chewed out a group of operational researchers at an international conference in Rome for being incomprehensible. "You have failed to educate the users of your talents to the potential you offer," he said. "Your studies, analyses, and reports are couched in tables that sales, operations, and maintenance personnel cannot comprehend."

Full-time Job

Whelan's work is a concrete example of the truth in a crack by Prof. Sidney Alexander of MIT—formerly economist for Columbia Broadcasting System—that the economist who understands marginal analysis has a "full-time job in undoing the work of the accountant." This is so, Alexander holds, because the practices of accountants—and of most businesses—are permeated with cost allocation directed at average, rather than marginal, costs.

In any complex business, there's likely to be a big difference between the costs of each company activity as it's carried on the accounting books and the marginal or "true" costs that can determine whether or not the activity should be undertaken.

Marginal Analysis in a Nutshell

Problem: Shall Continental run an extra daily flight from City X to City Y ?

The facts: Fully-allocated costs of this flight $4,500

Out-of-pocket costs of this flight $2,000

Flight should gross......................$3,100

Decision: Run the flight. It will add $1,100 to net profit—because it will add $3,100 to revenues and only $2,000 to costs. Overhead and other costs, totaling $2,500 [$4,500 minus $2,000], would be incurred whether the flight is run or not. Therefore, fully-allocated or "average" costs of $4,500 are not relevant to this business decision. It's the out-of-pocket or "marginal" costs that count.

The difficulty comes in applying the simple "textbook" marginal concept to specific decisions. If the economist is unwilling to make some bold simplifications, the job of determining "true" marginal costs may be highly complex, time-wasting, and too expensive. But even a rough application of marginal principles may come closer to the right answer for business decision-makers than an analysis based on precise average-cost data.

Proving that this is so demands economists who can break the crust of corporate habits and show concretely why the typical manager's response—that nobody ever made a profit without meeting all costs—is misleading and can reduce profits. To be sure, the whole business cannot make a profit unless average costs are met; but covering average costs should not determine whether any particular activity should be undertaken. For this would unduly restrict corporate decisions and cause managements to forgo opportunities for extra gains.

Approach

Management overhead at Continental is pared to the bone, so Whelan often is thrown such diverse problems as soothing a ruffled city council or planning the specifications for the plane the line will want to fly in 1970. But the biggest slice of his time goes to schedule planning—and it is here that the marginal concept comes most sharply into focus.

Whelan's approach is this: He considers that the bulk of his scheduled flights have to return at least their fully allocated costs. Overhead, depreciation, insurance are very real expenses and must be covered. The out-

of-pocket approach comes into play, says Whelan, only after the line's basic schedule has been set.

"Then you go a step farther," he says, and see if adding more flights will contribute to the corporate net. Similarly, if he's thinking of dropping a flight with a disappointing record, he puts it under the marginal microscope: "If your revenues are going to be more than your out-of-pocket costs, you should keep the flight on."

By "out-of-pocket costs" Whelan means just that: the actual dollars that Continental has to pay out to run a flight. He gets the figure not by applying hypothetical equations but by circulating a proposed schedule to every operating department concerned and finding out just what extra expenses it will entail. If a ground crew already on duty can service the plane, the flight isn't charged a penny of their salary expense. There may even be some costs eliminated in running the flight; they won't need men to roll the plane to a hangar, for instance, if it flies on to another stop.

Most of these extra flights, of course, are run at off-beat hours, mainly late at night. At times, though, Continental discovers that the hours aren't so unpopular after all. A pair of night coach flights on the Houston-San Antonio-El Paso-Phoenix-Los Angeles leg, added on a marginal basis, have turned out to be so successful that they are now more than converting fully allocated costs.

Alternative

Whelan uses an alternative cost analysis closely allied with the marginal concept in drawing up schedules. For instance, on his 11:11 p.m. flight from Colorado Springs to Denver and a 5:20 a.m. flight the other way, Continental uses Viscounts that, though they carry some cargo, often go without a single passenger. But the net cost of these flights is less than would be the rent for overnight hangar space for the Viscount at Colorado Springs.

And there's more than one absolute-loss flight scheduled solely to bring passengers to a connecting Continental long-haul flight; even when the loss on the feeder service is considered a cost on the long-haul service, the line makes a net profit on the trip.

Continental's data handling system produces weekly reports on each flight, with revenues measured against both out-of-pocket and fully allocated costs. Whelan uses these to give each flight a careful analysis at least once a quarter. But those added on a marginal basis get the fine-tooth-comb treatment monthly.

The business on these flights tends to be useful as a leading indicator, Whelan finds, since the off-peak traffic is more than normally sensitive to economic trends and will fall off sooner than that on the popular-hour flights. When he sees the night coach flights turning in consistently poor showings, it's a clue to lower his projections for the rest of the schedule.

Unorthodox

There are times, though, when the decisions dictated by the most expert marginal analysis seem silly at best, and downright costly at worst. For example, Continental will have two planes converging at the same time on Municipal Airport in Kansas City, when the new schedules take effect.

This is expensive because, normally, Continental doesn't have the facilities in K.C. to service two planes at once; the line will have to lease an extra fuel truck and hire three new hands—at a total monthly cost of $1,800.

But, when Whelan started pushing around proposed departure times in other cities to avoid the double landing, it began to look as though passengers switching to competitive flights leaving at choicer hours, would lose Continental $10,000 worth of business each month. The two flights will be on the ground in K.C. at the same time.

Full Work Week

This kind of scheduling takes some 35% of Whelan's time. The rest of his average work week breaks down this way: 25% for developing near-term, point-to-point traffic forecasts on which schedules are based; 20% in analyzing rates—Whelan expects to turn into a quasi-lawyer to plead Continental's viewpoint before the Civil Aeronautics Board; 20% on long-range forecasts and the where-should-we-go kind of planning that determines both which routes the line goes after and which it tries to shed. (Whelan's odd jobs in promotion, public relations, and general management don't fit into that time allotment; he says they "get stuck on around the side.")

The same recent week he was working on the data for his Kansas City double-landing problem, for instance, he was completing projections for the rest of 1963 so that other departments could use them for budget making, and was scrutinizing actions by Trans World Airlines, Inc., and Braniff Airways, Inc. TWA had asked CAB approval for special excursion fares from Eastern cities to Pacific Coast terminals; Whelan decided the plan worked out much the same as the economy fare on Continental's three-class service, so will neither oppose nor match the excursion deal. Braniff had just doubled its order—to 12—for British Aircraft Corp.'s 111 jets. Whelan was trying to figure out where they were likely to use the small planes, and what effect they would have on Continental's share of competing routes in Texas and Oklahoma.

At the same time, Whelan was meeting with officials of Frontier Airlines and Trans-Texas, coordinating the CAB-ordered takeover by the feeder lines of 14 stops Continental is now serving with leased DC-3s.

And he was struggling, too, with a knotty problem in consumer economics: He was trying to sell his home on Denver's CherryVale Drive and buy one in Los Angeles, where Continental will move its headquarters this summer. ■

QUESTIONS

1. Test whether you have grasped economist Chris Whelan's reasoning in the table titled "Marginal Analysis in a Nutshell" by answering the following similar question:

   Suppose Allstar Airlines flies between Phoenix and Las Vegas. It leases its planes on a year-long contract, at a cost that averages out to $4,050 per flight. Other costs—fuel, flight attendants, etc.—amount to $5,950 per flight. The average number of passengers is 150 per flight at a ticket price of $50. Is shutdown appropriate at this point? Explain your reasoning carefully.

2.   a. What examples from the article illustrate how "marginalism" can be applied?
     b. What two or three other examples can you think of?

This classic article by Thomas Edison on his marketing of light bulbs emphasizes that marginal cost rather than average cost is decisive in determining the profitability of additional sales. The article discusses how Edison raised his profits by selling light bulbs in Europe at a price below his "cost of production" (but above his "increased cost of production").

On Average And Marginal Cost

By THOMAS EDISON

I was the first manufacturer in the United States to adopt the idea of dumping surplus goods upon the foreign market. Thirty years ago my balance sheet showed me that I was not making much money. My manufacturing plant was not running to its full capacity. I couldn't find a market for my products. Then I suggested that we undertake to run our plant on full capacity and sell the surplus products in foreign markets at less than the cost of production. Every one of my associates opposed me. I had my experts figure out how much it would add to the cost of operating the plant if we increased this production 25 percent. The figures showed that we could increase the production 25 percent at an increased cost of only about 2 percent. On this basis I sent a man to Europe who sold lamps there at a price less than the cost of production in Europe.

QUESTIONS

1. Considering the cost concepts of microeconomics, what does Edison mean by
   a. "Cost of production"?
   b. "Increased cost" of production?

2. Could Edison's profits rise from selling additional output
   a. "At less than the cost of production"?
   b. At less than the "increased cost" of the production? Briefly explain both answers.

The Wall Street Journal, December 20, 1911. Reprinted by permission of the Wall Street Journal, © Dow Jones & Company, Inc. 1911 All rights reserved worldwide. (We wish to thank Professor Woody Studenmund of Occidental College for bringing this article to our attention.)

This article discusses the market for luxury cruises in the United States, and it deals with long-run entry and exit of firms. The article notes that firms in this industry are ordering many more ships in response to current and anticipated demand. Some commentators fear "overcapacity" and "over-entry" in the future. In addition, there are many quotations about "supply exceeding demand" in the future, with little apparent recognition of the role of price in balancing these forces.

More May Be Too Much

By ROBERT E. DALLOS

NEW YORK—Something might have to be done about the berth rate.

That's because so many bottles of champagne are being hurled at the bows of new cruise ships, sending them sliding down the ways. And, while cruising out of American ports is booming, there is a danger that before long there might be more liners than passengers to fill them.

It is a trend that will probably result in cheaper cruises for vacationers, but it could spell doom for some cruise companies.

"Overall, the cruise industry is expanding too fast," said Oivind Mathisen, editor and publisher of Cruise Industry News, a newsletter published in New York. "But those companies which have the marketing muscle and market support are likely to succeed, while the weaker lines—those not strong financially who don't have a clear marketing focus—may experience some rough seas ahead."

Cruise line operators deny that there are any real danger signals. They say public demand for cruises will continue to keep pace with capacity and that no real glut will develop.

Einar Kloster, chairman of Miami-based Kloster Cruise Ltd., owner of Norwegian Cruise Line and Royal Viking Line and a subsidiary of a Norwegian holding company, said, "As [ship] operators, we would not be very intelligent if we closed our eyes and said there will never be an overcapacity. But we still see a steady growth in the market. This industry is capacity-driven. Every time a new ship comes on, the base is widened."

Others tend to agree.

"So far, the rate of building has been pretty much in sync with the demand growth," said James G. Godsman, president of the Cruise Lines International Assn., a trade group representing 33 cruise lines serving North America. "Any time you have a period of building, you are going to have periods where you are going to have a little bit of excess supply, and there are going to be periods when you will have a little bit of undersupply. Right now, there is a little bit of excess."

But, for now, the figures look good for the industry. The association says 3 million passengers took cruises from American ports in 1987 and 3.5 million more are expected this year.

Tim Harris, president of Los Angeles-based Princess Cruises, noted that "in any business, from time to time there develops an imbalance between demand and supply. Whether there is a short-term imbalance [in the cruise business] will be determined by the economy."

But Princess seemingly has faith that more good times for the industry lie ahead. It is negotiating with a foreign shipyard for construction of a ship similar to its Royal Princess for delivery in 1991.

Other lines are also moving quickly to increase capacity: Before the end of this year, a dozen new ships for the American cruise market will have entered service. Eight more new ships are to begin cruising next year, and there will be 10 more in 1990 and four more in 1991. The 1988 newcomers include Royal Caribbean Cruise Lines' Sovereign of the Seas, which went into service in January and carries more cruise passengers than any ship in history: 2,250.

In times of emergency, of course, passenger ships can be modified to carry much greater numbers. According to the book "The Great Liners" by Melvin Maddocks, the greatest number of people embarked on one vessel was the 16,683 soldiers that the famed Queen Mary carried on one World War II voyage from New York to Scotland in July, 1943. The liner's normal passenger capacity was 1,904.

The Sovereign might not hold its cruise passenger capacity record for long. Among ships in the planning stages is one called the Ultimate Dream, which would carry 3,000 passengers. Another, the Phoenix, would be able to accommodate 5,000.

40 New Ships

The shipbuilding frenzy has been going on for some time.

According to Cruise Lines International Assn., the decade ending in 1989 will be "the most prolific in a generation" for shipbuilding, and 1988 will be the decade's busiest year. Forty new ships will have made their debuts in the 1980–89 period, according to CLIA.

Almost all of the major cruise lines have either just taken delivery or are expecting one or more liners in the near future. Los Angeles-based Sitmar Cruises, for example, is awaiting three new $150-million vessels beginning next January. And it seems clear that they will be needed to meet the demand: Observers say that about one-fifth of all cruise passengers come from California.

The first of Sitmar's new liners, the 1,470-passenger Fair Majesty, is under construction by the Chantiers de l'Atlantique shipyard in St. Nazaire, France, and will be delivered early next year. The other two, as yet unnamed, are being built in Italy and will be delivered in 1990 and 1991. The three ships will boost Sitmar's total passenger capacity by a whopping 265%, according to William L. Smith, the company's senior vice president of sales and marketing. Sitmar already has three ships serving the North American market.

Miami-based Carnival Cruise Lines, already the nation's biggest with seven ships serving the Caribbean and the Mexican Riviera, will add three new 2,050-passenger vessels beginning next year: the Fantasy, the Ecstasy and the Sensation. The 6,150 berths will boost the line's capacity by 75%, according to Bob Dickinson, senior vice president for sales and marketing.

Sophisticated Consumer

According to a study by Cruise Industry News, by the end of 1988 alone, the number of cruise ship berths to be marketed in the United States will grow by 11%, to 80,183. And that, the publication said, will result in a 30% industrywide over-supply of space by the year-end.

[A] If the supply and demand projections (based on confirmed orders for new berths) materialize, along with an increase of only 5% in demand, the newsletter added, the oversupply will rise to 32.5% in 1990 and 33% in 1991. Worse yet, if all the ships planned but for which contracts have not yet been signed are actually built, the oversupply might rise as high as 45% by 1992.

Competition is forcing the cruise operators to order all the new liners. "The most sophisticated consumer in the world is the American consumer," Kloster said. "They require that the major cruise lines have the latest and the best." (The average life of a cruise ship is 30 years, shipping executives say.)

Another reason for the surge in cruise shipbuilding is the advantageous financing the operators are getting. Foreign shipyards are building all of the ships being constructed for U.S. cruise lines—in such places as Finland, France, Italy, Germany, Japan and South Korea.

Many of these countries, to keep workers employed, subsidize their shipyards, which in turn pass the benefits along to their customers in the form of lower prices and low interest rates on loans.

Few of the cruise ship companies serving U.S. ports are American-owned, and most of the ships are registered in such places as Panama, Liberia and the Bahamas, mainly for tax reasons. Every so often, the foreign registration causes concerns about safety because U.S. regulators are powerless in such cases. But the head of the National Transportation Safety Board said recently that his agency is studying the U.S. responsibility for cruise ship safety.

If there is to be a cruise liner glut, the worst of it is expected in the early 1990s. It could create bankruptcies and consolidations of cruise lines and a bonanza of lower rates, special rates and discounts for cruise passengers.

"While the oversupply will make things tough for the cruise lines, it will create a paradise for passengers," said Mathisen of Cruise Industry News. "Prices will be drastically reduced. Travelers will have their pick."

It is estimted that if demand is to keep up with the building of cruise ships, the market must continue to grow by about 10% a year over the next five years.

However, a recent study by Temple, Barker & Sloane, a Massachusetts research firm specializing in the cruise industry, concluded that supply will outpace demand through 1992 and that this will result in a decline in the industry's average load factor to 73%, compared to the current average of about 90%.

In 1992, the growth of demand will begin to exceed supply growth as the rate of new ships going into service declines. But it will still take until the year 2000 for the cruise industry to recover to a load factor of 77%, the research firm says.

Business Brisk

For the present, however, business is brisk.

According to Kloster, the two companies that he heads have increased their capacity by a third with the recent introduction of Norwegian Cruise Line's 1,500-

passenger Seaward and Royal Viking Line's 740-passenger Royal Viking Sun. Kloster said load factors are running at about 103%—which is possible because ship occupancy is based on two in a cabin but there are pull-down berths in many cabins.

Cruise operators contend emphatically that there are so many people "out there" who might take cruises that no serious oversupply of ships will develop and that the market they can tap is vast.

"The industry has demonstrated that it has a very high growth rate," said Harvey Katz, shipping analyst with the Salomon Bros. investment firm. So far, he added, cruise line operators have reached only a few of the Americans who, according to statistical analysis, might go on cruises.

Shipping lines maintain that only about 4% of the more than 30 million people who would be able to take a cruise (according to such criteria as age and income) have ever done so.

"There have been misconceptions that cruising has been for the old, the overweight and for people who like to be bored," Godsman, head of the CLIA trade group, said. "Today's cruise is anything but."

Observers say that, although there are millions of potential cruise customers waiting on land, the cruise companies must put great effort into promoting their product. And many are turning increasingly to television advertising.

"Unless major changes are made in the way cruise lines sell themselves," said Jay Lewis, who heads Market Scope, a Miami research firm specializing in the cruise industry, "their growth in popularity as a holiday option may stagnate, and the industry will be left with severe overcapacity on its hands into the 1990s.

But officials of many lines insist that even an economic downturn will not greatly affect the popularity of cruising. Demand continued to grow during the recession of the early 1980s, they point out.

One major reason that cruising is so popular is that it often provides good value for the money. For as little as $175 to $200 per day, passengers can get air fare to the port where the voyage begins, room, food, entertainment and visits to several attractive ports.

"A land-based vacation . . . can cost $1,000 a day," said Ram Capoor, shipping analyst with Morgan Stanley & Co., a New York investment firm. "One can take Carnival Cruise—the Chevrolet of the industry—for $1,000 a week." ∎

QUESTIONS

1. How would you illustrate the current situation in the market for luxury cruises in the United States? Illustrate with appropriate diagrams for the industry and for the "typical" firm, assuming that this industry can be described by the model of perfect competition. (For the purposes of this and the remaining questions, assume that the luxury cruise industry is characterized by constant costs.)

2. Use your diagrams to explain what will happen in this industry in the long run, assuming that "supply growth outpaces demand growth," at least until 1992.

3. Now consider passage A:
   a. In the forecast of the increase in "demand," what do you think is the projected change in price?
   b. Indicate whether you think each of the following values in 1992 will be higher, lower, or the same as the values assumed by *Cruise Industry News:*

   (1) The price of luxury cruises
   (2) The "oversupply" of luxury cruise berths
   Briefly support your answers.

4. This article has dealt with the possible entry of new producers in the long run. The article on mink farming in Selection 8 ("Mink Farming Is Growing More Scarce as Costs Rise and Fur Demand Declines") dealt explicitly with the exit of producers in the long run. Please refer to passage G in that article in answering the following question:
   a. Has the mink farming industry reached a new long-run equilibrium? Explain why or why not.
   b. Show on a carefully labeled diagram why a mink producer might continue to produce even if this person observed, as in passage G, that "we're losing about $3 a pelt on our mutations."

This article illustrates the shutdown decision and involves a
real case of long-run exit in response to a decrease in demand.

Lag in Tanker Business Puts the Squeeze
On Builders and Owners—as Well as Banks

By JOHN D. WILLIAMS

Cloverton Shipping Co., a Liberian-registered concern
owned by U.S. interests, recently canceled orders with
a Swedish shipbuilder for two 360,000-ton oil tankers.
The reason: inability to line up charter customers for
1977.

In West Germany, a major bank recently fore-
closed on a 109,000-ton, seven-year-old tanker, taking
it from its Norwegian operator and selling it to a Greek
concern. The new owner was granted a two-year moratorium on principal payments under the new mortgage.

And in Oslo, Hilmar Reksten, a major shipowner,
defaulted on orders for a total of six big tankers that
were to be built there by the Aker Group. An arbitration
panel recently awarded Aker the equivalent of about
$67 million in cancellation payments for four of the
ships. Mr. Reksten has been severely hurt by low tanker
rates and soaring operating costs.

As these examples suggest, the oil-tanker business
isn't exactly booming. Overcapacity troubles had been
predicted by experts as long ago as 1970, but it took the
Mideast oil boycott, the quadrupling of oil prices since
October 1973 and international economic woes to bring
it all to a head.

Tankers Orders Canceled

Of the world-wide fleet of 4,000 tankers, 433 are
laid up in port with no business—a record number. In
the Persian Gulf, some 20 ships are riding at anchor,
waiting for cargo that may or may not materialize.
Many of the tankers that do have oil to carry are poking
along at slower than normal speeds to save fuel. All
told, shipowners have canceled orders for 100 tankers
since last November.

**[A] Most observers figure that order cancellations
and increased scrappings by shipowners will eventually
bring things back into line, probably within three years.
But in the meantime, everyone agrees it's going to be**

**tough sailing for shipbuilders and owners, as well as for
the array of international banks that have lent money
to the industry. Warns J. A. Waage, an executive vice
president of New York's Manufacturers Hanover Trust
Co., "The (tanker) situation is one of the biggest clouds
on the horizon of international banking."**

That certainly wasn't the case in 1973, when there
was an unprecedented demand for tankers to haul oil to
the U.S., Europe and Japan, where industrial production was running high. Charter rates were at record
highs, with some independent owners grossing as much
as $10 million on a single voyage. With those kinds of
figures at stake, bankers were more than eager to lend
money for new ships. And a record 105 million tons of
tankers—equal to over 1,000 tankers of average size—
were ordered that year. That was double the previous
record in 1972.

But following the Mideast oil boycott, oil consumption in the U.S., Western Europe and Japan fell
by about 5% in 1974, after growing at a 10% rate in
1973. The work skidded from boom to recession. And
the world-wide tanker-fleet capacity rose by about 18%
in 1974. (The lead time for a big tanker is about two
years, and previously ordered ships are still being turned
out at the rate of six a week.)

Some banks have had to make loan concessions to
their shipbuilder clients. Last month, for example,
Chase Manhattan Bank agreed to substitute a six-year,
$65 million term loan to Seatrain Lines Inc. of New
York without any payment of principal in the first two
years. It replaced a $65 million short-term loan that has
been overdue since early 1973. Seatrain builds tankers
for others and also operates its own oil tankers and
ocean freighters.

A Not-So-Halcyon Tanker

Bankers Trust Co., New York, holds a $19.5 mil-
lion second mortgage on one of the world's most famous tankers, the 226,700-ton Halcyon the Great, sold
at a court auction recently in London to a Hong Kong
shipping man. The tanker had previously been owned

by a diversified British travel company that went bankrupt last August. And in a well-publicized sea chase, the Royal Canadian Mounted Police tried in vain to slap a creditor's lien on the ship last October while it was trying to escape Canadian waters.

Overall estimates of international banks' outstanding loans to the industry are difficult to obtain, and most major U.S. and London bankers flatly refuse to discuss the matter. But one European banking source notes that many oil-tanker loans are secured through government credits or similar governmental help. He estimates that at most, possibly a half-dozen European banks, all of them secondary lending institutions, are overcommitted in tanker loans. Some, he concedes, could sink as a result of an unsecured loan to a foundering tanker man. But so far that hasn't happened.

Neither have any shipyards closed down, though one New York banking official predicts that "tanker assembly lines will grind to a halt by the second quarter of next year." The big Japanese shipyards, such as the Nagasaki facility of Mitsubishi Heavy Industries Ltd., produce about half the world's oil tankers. But spokesmen for the Japanese concerns decline to discuss the situation.

One large U.S. shipbuilder that has been affected is Todd Shipyards Corp., New York, which had a loss of $43.4 million in the fiscal year ended March 31. The company has halted a planned expansion of its Los Angeles yard because orders for eight 90,000-ton tankers were canceled. (The orders were canceled largely at Todd's request because they were on a fixed-price basis and Todd's costs were soaring.)

Unprofitable Rates

[B] Many owners are chartering out their tankers at rates far lower than what they need to cover operating expenses—just to keep their crews intact or simply to get their ships home for lay-up. Exxon Corp. reportedly just chartered for $900,000 a year a Japanese tanker that costs $2 million a year to operate. One reason for the seemingly illogical deal: Japanese union rules require the owner to pay its seagoing crew its full wages whether or not the ship is employed.

[C] Meanwhile, scrapping of old tankers is easing some of the pressure on the market. In the first five months of this year 135 tankers totaling 3.6 million tons were scrapped, well above the 1.9 million tons scrapped in all of 1974. Scrap concerns in Taiwan and India pay $95 to $98 a ton for scrap metal. And some ship brokers say buyers currently have a chance to make a profitable two-way play on a tanker purchase: for chartering if the market improves or for scrapping if it doesn't.

Indeed, there are plenty of tanker bargains around. Arne Naess & Co. Inc., a New York ship broker, says prices today are about 10% of what they were at the peak in June 1973. Brokers report that the Liberian-registered Benjamin Coates, a 50,000-ton tanker built in 1960 was recently sold for $1.1 million, only slightly above what its scrap value would be.

QUESTIONS

1. Consider passage A, and assume that this is a constant cost industry: Draw the industry demand and supply curves for oil tanker services now and three years from now as well as the situation of the "typical" tanker operator.

2. Consider passage B: Explain clearly why the Japanese shipowner was profit maximizing even though he took losses.

This article on the disintegration of the NCAA's monopoly over television rights for college sports offers a clear contrast between monopoly and competition. Price, output, profit, and welfare effects are all readily apparent in the article.

A Supremely Unsettling Smorgasbord

By WILLIAM TAAFFE

For a vivid glimpse of the new college football world that the Georgia Bulldogs, Oklahoma Sooners and U.S. Supreme Courterbacks have wrought, we take you to, of all places, the Hub. That's right, Boston. Not the most storied of college football cities. However, thanks to the Supreme Court decision that ended the NCAA's control over college football telecasts, it's now a typical all-American viewing center.

In Boston this fall, Harvard physicists will be able to watch Crimson games on PBS; subway alumni in the bars of Southie will be able to choose from among at least seven games between noon and midnight; and Notre Dame grads will be able to second-guess almost every Gerry Faust decision live and in color. In Boston, as elsewhere, this is going to be a dream season for college football fans. Not everyone is going to watch every game, of course, but let's imagine a possible Saturday for a Bostonian.

Say you've just driven out to the in-laws' in Marblehead. No need for small talk. Get right to that tube. At noon, when most schools and conferences have agreed to air their regional packages, you've got your pick of the Ivy League on PBS, a Boston College, Pitt or Syracuse game on another channel and Notre Dame or Penn State on yet a third. In-laws feed you at 2:45. At three, it's the big national games on the networks. Here comes Keith Jackson on ABC with a game from the CFA, the umbrella group that represents all 105 Division 1-A schools except those in the Big Ten and Pac-10. CBS has those two conferences, and sure enough, Gary Bender is on right now with a Pac-10 game. Whew, 6:30! Hungry! In-laws left dinner for you in the oven. Forget washing the dishes because the big cable game will be on at seven. You have your choice of either another CFA game on ESPN or an SEC matchup on

WTBS, the Ted Turner superstation. In-laws in the sack by 10, so leave quietly. Patriots on tomorrow.

One Bostonian who's happier than a clam is Tom Mulvey, president of the Notre Dame Alumni Club of Greater Boston. To see each week's Irish game in the past, he and his 500 dues-paying members had to a) have access to cable and b) hunt through ESPN's rerun listings to learn which day a tape would be rolled. Mulvey now hopes to stage live-TV viewing parties almost every Saturday, complete with hats, T shirts and other shamrocky paraphernalia. "Yes, you could say I'm happy," he says.

Seems like a perfect world, doesn't it? The only problem is that one school in Boston with everything going for it will make far less money from TV this season than last. That school is Boston College, a.k.a. Doug Flutie U. Like the great majority of the Division 1-A schools, BC has abruptly discovered that the Supreme Court decision is no blessing.

BC offers a striking illustration of how a college can be worse off under the new math precisely when it should be wallowing in riches. Flutie, who in three years has brought the Eagles out of the dark ages in football, is a front-runner for the Heisman Trophy. Boston College will be on national TV at least three times—Sept. 8 against Alabama (ABC), Sept. 22 against North Carolina (ESPN) and Nov. 23 against Miami (CBS). BC has a good team, a refurbished stadium and fans who are yell-aholics. If the bloom is suddenly off the BC rose *with* Flutie, what's going to happen once he graduates? "It's a little scary," says athletic director Bill Flynn.

Last season, four regular-season TV appearances earned BC $1,585,000. Only Alabama, Texas and UCLA took in more television bucks. This year Boston College expected to clean up again, but then the Supreme Court acted in response to the action filed by Georgia and Oklahoma, and the game changed. With Big Ten and Pac-10 schools parting ways with the CFA, the TV seller's market became a buyer's market, and the networks held the trump cards. Why should they pay top dollar when they no longer were the exclusive carriers of college football? An anticipated $800,000 payment to BC from CBS for the Miami game became $400,000. An expected $700,000 from ABC for the Alabama game became $250,000. Boston College will receive about $100,000 per game for the three or four games its regional syndicator, Katz Sports, will send around the East. The bottom line? The Eagles will be on television about 50% more often than in 1983 for about 50% less money.

NCAA president John Toner, admittedly not an impartial observer, points out that the Supreme Court decision may lead to a self-perpetuating "superconference" of TV schools that corners the market on money, athletes and national exposure. According to Eagle coach Jack Bicknell, because BC's a new kid on the TV block it will never be one of those schools. "Yes, we have an outstanding quarterback and, yes, there's a lot of interest in us this year, but down the road I just don't know," he says. "I'm more concerned with how many people are in the stands. Yes, we're going to be on TV more, but that to me is not good for the long haul."

So much for the brave new world as seen from Boston. The picture is much the same elsewhere. **[A] The regional/network/cable TV dance will go on every Saturday in every corner of the country. It has become abundantly clear that only a handful of schools—most notably a few in the Pac-10 plus Penn State—will take home more TV money this season than last. ABC and CBS, which last year paid a total of $62.5 million for college football and this year are paying $20 million, have won the money game.** Oklahoma may have to rent out its stadium to the USFL next spring to raise revenue. But Oklahoma and Georgia won't get any sympathy from their NCAA brethren. **[B] Says Washington State coach Jim Walden, who like most college officials believes Georgia and Oklahoma should have left well enough alone, "I can understand glut and greed, but I don't understand stupidity. I think this [lawsuit] will go down in history as one of the stupidest things ever done."**

[C] For the viewer, however, it may go down as the biggest bonanza since Congress exempted the NFL from antitrust. Have a nice time at the in-laws. ■

QUESTIONS

Consider the market for televised college football games, in which TV stations buy television rights either from the NCAA (before the Supreme Court decision cited in the article) or from individual college conferences (after the decision).

1. Use a supply and demand diagram for televised NCAA football games to contrast the NCAA monopoly equilibrium before the Supreme Court decision with a competitive equilibrium after the decision. Assume a constant cost of televising each game.
2. Consider passage A:
   a. When the market shifted from its monopoly equilibrium to its competitive equilibrium, was the demand for televised games elastic or inelastic? How can you tell?
   b. Suppose that, during its monopoly era, the NCAA had hired you as a consultant to help maximize NCAA profits. If you had come to the same conclusion as in part **a** concerning the elasticity of demand at the NCAA's existing output level, would you have suggested that the NCAA raise, lower, or leave unchanged the number of televised games? Briefly support your recommendation.
3. Consider passages B and C:
   a. Why does passage B make economic sense from the perspective of the sellers' side of the market?
   b. Why does passage C make economic sense from the perspective of the consumers' side of the market?
   c. In your diagram from question 1, indicate areas that illustrate the concepts relevant to your answers for parts **a** and **b**.

This is a very polished article written by an economist who attempts to describe the "oligopolistic" market for principles of economics textbooks. It is the closest we come to including a "readings" article, as opposed to a "popular press" article that illustrates a key economic principle. The article also analyzes the classic example of profit versus sales maximization in a monopoly by discussing the conflicting pricing strategies of a book-publishing monopoly and an author whose royalties are based on total sales revenue.

The Market for Principles of Economics Texts

Your instructor tells you what book to buy. Your campus bookstore is the only place that sells it. The only real choice you are likely to have in buying the economics text that will teach you about choices in competitive markets is the possible option of buying, for something close to the price of a new book, one that someone else has marked up.

There are choices in the market for introductory economics texts; the only problem is that you don't make many of them.

"It's a health-care decision," observes George Lobell, the economics editor at Scott, Foresman. The "doctor" picks the text, and the "patient" is more or less obliged to buy it.

Introductory economics texts are marketed in an oligopolistic market, one facing increasingly vigorous competition from a well-organized used-book market.

While there are roughly 50 introductory texts in print, the market is dominated by only a handful.

Market Leaders

The leader is Campbell McConnell's *Economics,* now in its tenth edition. The book, which first appeared on the market in 1963, holds roughly 15 percent of a market estimated to be about one million books per year.

Mr. McConnell, an economist at the University of Nebraska, captured the market lead with his 6th edition in 1973. The previous leader was Massachusetts Institute of Technology economist Paul Samuelson, whose text had led the market for more than two decades. Both texts are published by McGraw-Hill, the leading publisher in the market.

Mr. Samuelson's book, *Economics,* first published in 1948, set the standard for introductory economics texts. He was the first to put macroeconomics at the beginning of the book and to integrate the Keynesian model into the analysis. Subsequent texts, including Mr. McConnell's, have followed the basic outline established by Mr. Samuelson 40 years ago.

The success of Mr. Samuelson's text has been extraordinary. It has sold four million copies in its 12 editions. Mr. Samuelson wrote the book, he says, at the request of his department chairman at MIT.

"He came to me and said he'd give me some time off to write a text that we could use for our students at MIT. They had to take economics, and we couldn't find a suitable text in the market. He told me to cover anything I wanted and to make it as short as I wanted.

"That project eventually ended up taking about three years of hard work. Several publishers wanted the final product—I picked McGraw-Hill because it had published (Joseph) Schumpeter, and because it didn't have another strong principles text. The book was a success from the beginning."

The competitiveness of the market is suggested by the low market shares of the leaders. Thomas Horton, who was the economics editor at McGraw-Hill during the 1960's when "Samuelson" was almost synonymous with "economics," recalls that even during that period the book never had more than a 25 percent market share.

Copycats?

Mr. Horton now heads Thomas Horton and Daughters, a publisher of college texts (the name of the firm was the brainchild of Milton Friedman). He argues that current introductory texts fit in the Samuelson mold because anything that is radically different won't sell. "There's no question that innovation does not pay off in this market," he says.

Al Goodyear, who started his own publishing firm in 1968 and sold it in 1981 to Scott, Foresman, argues that part of the similarity in texts comes from an effort to be complete. "A text has to have everything everyone else has, plus something different," he says. This effort to be comprehensive accounts for the large size of economics texts; most are 800 to 1,000 pages in length.

"Professors often tell me they want a shorter, less encyclopedic text," Mr. Samuelson says, "but when one comes on the market, they don't buy it. Besides, the marginal cost of going with a 900 page text instead of a 500 page one is very low, so there's not much incentive to cut length."

Sales figures of competing texts are not available; publishers guard them carefully. The result, says Milton Spencer, the author of a text published by Worth Publishers and an economist at Wayne State University, is that people in the industry know very little about their own market.

Mr. Spencer's text, *Contemporary Economics,* is regarded as being part of the pack of major texts trailing McConnell. The pack includes Mr. Samuelson's book, now coauthored with William Nordhaus, as well as texts by William Baumol and Alan Blinder, Roger Miller, Richard Lipsey and Peter Steiner, Edwin Dolan, and Roy Ruffin and Paul Gregory. Mr. Spencer estimates that each of these has about five percent of the market, suggesting annual sales of about 50,000.

Used Books

Calculating shares is difficult because of the importance of the used book market. Industry officials generally agree that sales of a new book, or a new edition of a book, will fall 50 percent in the second year because of competition from used copies of the same book. Sales typically fall another 50 percent in the third year. "By the third year, your used books are doing better than you are," Mr. Goodyear observes.

Used books enter the market primarily when students sell them back to bookstores. Bookstores typically pay half the retail price for a book they can resell on their own campus. If the book is not being used again on a campus, it may be bought by a used book wholesaler that will pay a third or less of the original retail price. These books are then distributed to campus bookstores where they typically sell for 75 percent of the original price.

The hostility of publishers to the used book market runs deep. As the economics editor at one leading publishing house puts it, "those guys (used book wholesalers) have a legal right to do what they do, but I question the morality of it.

"They're ripping us off and they're ripping our authors off. They make money from our books, our work, and we don't collect a dime."

A little economics may ease the hostility. Because a student knows a text can be resold for as much as half the original price, he or she will be willing to pay more for it initially. This increases the demand for new texts.

The used book market thus pulls demand both ways. The expectation that a book can be resold raises demand for new books at the same time the availability of used books lowers demand.

Another channel through which books enter the used book market is the "complimentary copy" market.

As part of their marketing efforts, publishers typically send professors sample copies of their texts. After a professor has examined a book and decided not to use it, it has little further value to him or her. But it does have potential value to students to whom the text has been assigned. There are dozens of buyers who travel from campus to campus, buying sample copies of texts from professors and selling them to used book brokers.

Mr. Lobell says it is typical to send out six to seven thousand complimentary copies of a principles text and to have more than half come back to compete in the used book market.

On the demand side, then, texts face competition not only from other texts, but from themselves in their used incarnation. But what about the cost side?

Costs

Industry officials are reluctant to discuss publishing costs. But, in conversations with several publishers, *THE MARGIN* was able to obtain a rough breakdown of the cost of a principles text.

Most publishers suggest a retail price to college bookstores and then charge the bookstore 80 percent of this price for the book. For a $35 book, this means that the publisher receives $28.

Authors typically get a 15 percent royalty on the publisher's price, or $4.20 per book sold.

Overhead, marketing, and profits account for about $11. A typical target is a profit of 20 percent of wholesale price, but whether this is achieved depends on the success of the book. "Plant overhead," which includes composition and illustration, is about $5. The cost of printing a book, the unit binding cost, is about $4.50 in the output range of most leading texts. Editorial costs, including the fees paid to other professors to review manuscripts, add another $2.

Many publishers determine their price by adding up their costs and tacking on a margin for profit—the so-called "mark-up pricing" approach. The prices charged by rivals are considered as well.

As is common in oligopolies, text publishers keep a wary eye on each other's prices. They pay particular attention to the prices charged by McGraw-Hill, the firm generally regarded as the price leader in the industry.

Two years ago, prices for introductory economics texts were bunched at about $30. Then McGraw-Hill boosted its price for the McConnell text by a whopping $5. Other publishers followed suit the following year; prices are now about $35 for most texts.

Buyers might want to beware; McGraw-Hill has raised its prices again. The McConnell text now lists for $38, and the Samuelson-Nordhaus entry $41.

Demand and Price

Does price matter very much? There are, not surprisingly, two schools of thought.

Robert Tollison, the coauthor of a new principles text from Little, Brown and Company, suggests price could matter a great deal. "I think the demand is probably elastic. If a professor sees that a publisher's prices are out of line with the rest of the industry, he or she is going to be a lot less likely to use that publisher's book."

Joyce Riley, a sales representative for Addison-Wesley, a relatively new entrant in the market for principles texts, agrees. "Price is becoming a real issue—particularly at smaller schools. I've noticed a lot of concern at schools that have more commuter students."

Mr. Spencer, on the other hand, argues that the demand is inelastic with respect to price. He says most professors don't know what the price of a text is when they pick it. Price information is not included in the promotional materials professors get about texts.

[A] If demand is inelastic, it raises a problem. With inelastic demand, an increase in price would raise revenue. It would also reduce quantity demanded and reduce costs. It would, therefore, increase profits. A profit-maximizing firm would not charge a price in the inelastic range of its demand curve.

Mr. Spencer concludes that publishers do not seek to maximize profits. "I think publishers are sales maximizers, not profit maximizers, he says."

[B] If they are, it may answer a puzzle posed by the University of Chicago's George Stigler several years ago. Mr. Stigler noted that, since authors are paid a fixed percentage of total sales revenues, they should want publishers to charge a price that maximizes total revenue, not profits.

The difference is shown in Figure 1. Maximizing total revenue means selling books at the point that marginal revenue is zero and charging a price lower than the

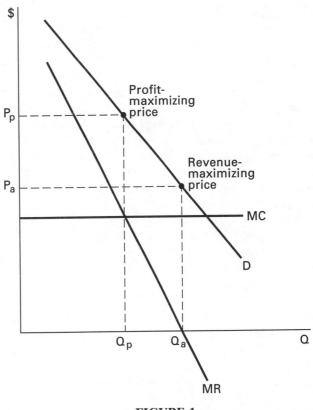

FIGURE 1

price that would maximize profit. The result should be a conflict between publishers and authors over pricing decisions, with authors seeking a price lower than the price a profit-maximizing firm should want. But in a survey of authors of economics texts, Mr. Stigler found no evidence of this sort of disagreement over publisher policies.

Mr. Lobell suggests that, in addition to the interest of authors in maximizing total revenues, the sales force of a publishing firm is seeking the same thing. While sales representatives earn a fixed salary, they get bonuses for exceeding their quotas of book sales.

That leads to strong internal pressure to hold prices down. Ms. Riley recalls that when her firm recently raised prices on one of its texts, "the sales reps screamed bloody murder."

Competition and increasing price awareness by professors help to keep prices down. So, as it turns out, do the interests of authors and salespeople. You might not know it, but you've got friends in the publishing industry. ◼

QUESTIONS

1. Why isn't the demand for a particular economics textbook perfectly inelastic? In your answer, refer to the article.
2. Consider passage A: Explain in your own words why "if demand is inelastic, it raises a problem." Be sure to explain exactly what the problem is here.
3. Consider passage B: According to Stigler's analysis, should the publisher and author want the book to be sold at the same price? If not, who wants a lower price? Why?
4. Refer to Figure 1 in the article:
   a. If publishers end up picking P_p, the profit-maximizing price, is the result efficient? Explain your answer.
   b. If publishers end up picking P_a, the sales-maximizing price, is this result efficient? Explain your answer.
   c. If neither of the above results in efficiency, which is better in this regard? Explain.
5. a. Do firms appear to compete on price in this market?
   b. What forms of nonprice competition are there in this market?
   c. What, if any, evidence is there that firms recognize their "mutual interdependence"? Explain.

This newspaper advertisement deals with the topic of price discrimination. The pricing policy described in the ad is a fairly typical business practice, and we have seen it in ads for cameras, computers, typewriters, refrigerators, and several other items.

Trade-A-Beta

RCA's advertisement for a Beta VCR appears on page 64.

QUESTIONS

1. How do you think the elasticity of demand of those who already have a VCR compares with those who do not? Explain your answer.
2. Based on your answer to question 1, why does RCA find its advertised policy preferable to a simple sale in which all buyers get a lower price?
3. List the conditions necessary for successful price discrimination. Do you think the situation in this ad meets these necessary conditions? Explain briefly.
4. Many college bookstores offer "discounts" to professors. How is such a policy similar to the one in this ad?

Courtesy of Thomson Consumer Electronics, Inc. Indianapolis, Indiana.

The "smoking gun" of a potential collusive agreement appears to be quite evident in this article. The core of the article consists of excerpts from a phone conversation between the presidents of American and Braniff Airlines. American's president, Robert Crandall, advocates two seemingly incompatible objectives, emphatically suggesting that both airlines should raise their fares on competing routes and also arguing that they should leave "no room for Delta."

American Air Accused of Bid to Fix Prices

By ROBERT E. TAYLOR and DEAN ROTBART

The Justice Department, in a civil antitrust suit, charged American Airlines and its president and chief operating officer, Robert L. Crandall, with attempting to monopolize airline routes by trying to fix prices with Braniff International Corp.

The suit accuses Mr. Crandall of seeking an agreement to raise fares 20%. The suit, filed in federal court in Dallas, claims that the attempt came in a telephone conversation between Mr. Crandall and Braniff President Howard Putnam on Feb. 1, 1982. According to the Justice Department, Mr. Putnam rejected the alleged offer.

In a prepared statement, American Airlines, the operating unit of AMR Corp., called the charge "entirely unjustified" and said that it and Mr. Crandall will "vigorously defend the suit, and fully expect to win." Albert V. Casey, American's chairman, said the company's board had monitored the situation closely and "has expressed full confidence in Mr. Crandall."

The lawsuit seeks an injunction barring Mr. Crandall for two years from serving American or any other scheduled airline as president, chief executive officer or in any other position with authority over prices. It doesn't seek any other sanctions against the airline.

The civil case comes in the wake of both criminal and civil antitrust investigations of the airline business, including American, Braniff and possibly other carriers. The investigations began about the same time that some Braniff officials and other industry employees claimed that American was using dirty tricks to try and force

Braniff out of business. At the time, fare wars between the two airlines were costing both companies a fortune.

Braniff filed last May under Chapter 11 of the federal Bankruptcy Code.

Elliott Seiden, a Justice Department attorney, said that the criminal grand jury probe was closed yesterday, the day the civil suit was filed. And department spokesman Mark Sheehan said "there is no intention to proceed with a criminal case in this matter." Officials declined to say whether the civil case stemmed from the grand jury investigation.

American contends that the Justice Department suit is based on "one isolated incident" in which, it alleges, Braniff's Mr. Putnam secretly taped a conversation with Mr. Crandall.

Without stating its source, the complaint includes a partial transcript of a telephone conversation allegedly between the two men. It quotes Mr. Crandall as saying, "I think it's dumb as hell . . . to sit here and pound the s--- out of each other and neither one of us making a (deleted) dime. . . . We can both live here and there ain't no room for Delta. But there's, ah, no reason that I can see, all right, to put both companies out of business."

After Mr. Putnam asks, "Do you have a suggestion for me?" the complaint says, Mr. Crandall replies, "Yes. I have a suggestion for you. Raise your goddamn fares 20%. I'll raise mine the next morning. . . . you'll make more money and I will too."

The transcript continues with Mr. Putnam saying, "We can't talk about pricing," to which Mr. Crandall retorts, "Oh bull----, Howard. We can talk about any goddamn thing we want to talk about."

American paraphrased the government as saying that Mr. Crandall was blaming poor revenues of both airlines on Braniff's "below-cost fares," and suggesting they be raised. American said Mr. Crandall's remarks were "an observation which had been made publicly by many leaders and analysts in the industry."

The complaint charges Mr. Crandall and American with attempting to monopolize business on routes between the Dallas-Fort Worth Airport and other airports that both airlines serve. The department estimated that revenues from those routes exceeded $434 million in 1981.

Antitrust attorneys noted that the charge was unusual. While a simple charge of price fixing is common, that offense exists only if two parties agree to it, attorneys said. But an attempt to monopolize can be either a civil or criminal charge, they said.

A Justice Department spokesman said the agency proceeds with criminal charges against an attempt to monopolize only under "the most extreme and unusual circumstances." He noted that "rarely are the issues so clear and simple" as to be appropriate for criminal prosecution. And he said prior cases haven't "directly" classified the conduct alleged in this case as a violation of that law, so the department decided to proceed with a civil case.

American asserted that "the government . . . reasons that, even though no agreement occurred, Mr. Crandall's alleged single comment amounted to an attempt to monopolize. The (government's) theory is both factually and legally unsupportable."

Joe Sims, a former deputy in the antitrust division, noted that raising prices wouldn't ordinarily help companies jointly monopolize a market, as price boosts would attract other companies into the business. But the complaint notes that entry into the routes surrounding the Dallas–Fort Worth airport has been restricted since 1981 because of the shortage of air-traffic controllers.

According to American, the department has said the investigation of dirty tricks against Braniff will continue as a civil investigation. This joins another civil probe into whether some airlines have been using their computerized scheduling systems to put competitors at a disadvantage.

Bitter Rivals

While it isn't clear exactly what role Braniff played in the Justice Department action against American and Mr. Crandall, Braniff has said previously that its officials had been interviewed by lawyers from the department's antitrust division. The two airlines were bitter rivals when Braniff was still flying, and harsh words have continued to fly back and forth between the two corporate staffs. American has been one of the most ardent opponents of a Braniff plan to lease or sell most of its assets to PSA Inc.

At one point, early last March, Mr. Crandall was quoted as saying that it would suit him to see the then-beleaguered Braniff "go out of business" so that American could start competing with "healthier airlines" that wouldn't cut fares "out of desperation." The remarks angered many people in the Dallas area, who depended on Braniff for jobs, business or transportation.

Mr. Crandall, 47 years old, has a reputation as a tough-talking executive who is admired by his peers, but who some say doesn't have much tact when it comes to dealing with the press or the public. Mr. Crandall, who has been president of American for just under three years, generally is credited with helping to bring the company's overhead costs down and improve the company's financial performance. ■

QUESTIONS

1. Concerning the conversation between American's president Crandall and Braniff's president Putnam:
   a. If Putnam had agreed to go along with Crandall's alleged suggestion, what would have happened to airline ticket prices in the Dallas area?
   b. Was Crandall's statement concerning the fate of Delta consistent with his pricing suggestion? Why or why not?
2. If Putnam had agreed with Crandall:
   a. Do you think evidence of the apparent collusive agreement would have been easy or hard to find? Explain briefly.
   b. For antitrust purposes, what difference does your answer to part **a** make?

In this article about the current problems encountered by cartels, all the major international commodity cartels except OPEC are mentioned. The article systematically lays out the inherent problems of cartels and indicates that in today's international markets, competition is the norm. It also offers a contrast between the demand elasticity facing a cartel and the elasticity facing a single cartel member.

Market Forces and Discord Stymie Cartels

By NEIL BEHRMANN

LONDON—The price-bolstering clout of the world's commodity cartels is evaporating amid discord among producing nations and the dominance of market forces.

"Commodity agreements are an endangered species," says Charles Young, director of research at Landell Mills Commodities Studies Ltd. Such accords were fashionable in the 1970s, he says, but policymakers today believe in "free markets and privatization."

Nearly a decade ago, more than 150 nations, rich and poor, wanted to devise a grand strategy to stabilize prices of 10 commodities and bolster cash flows of the Third World nations that produce raw materials. United Nations planners envisioned a "common fund" that would finance various pacts covering coffee, tea, cocoa, sugar, cotton, rubber, jute, sisal, tin and copper.

Despite six years of effort, however, the fund never materialized. And just one new pact, covering rubber, was negotiated.

Tin's international agreement dates from before World War II, and sugar, coffee and cocoa pacts existed before 1977 and have been renegotiated several times since then. Only cocoa and rubber are fully active now, though.

[A] Coffee's price-support mechanisms have been suspended more than a year while producing and consuming members argue about how to allocate export quotas. Although the International Coffee Organization's executive board meets this week in Bali, the panel isn't expected to decide the quota question before it meets in September at its London headquarters.

The International Sugar Agreement's price and quota functions lapsed in 1984 when members couldn't agree on export restrictions to support prices. And metal markets still suffer from the October 1985 collapse of the International Tin Council, which ran out of money by supporting prices far above market levels. Malaysia and Indonesia scuttled attempts to save the ITC early last year, delegates say, because the two nations weren't prepared to raise more money for support operations.

The spirit behind the international planning of 10 years ago, "is dead," says Robert Fish, managing director of Primary Commodity Research Ltd., a consulting firm. Noble efforts to bolster the economies of Third World nations have been overtaken by self-interest, he says.

"Some years ago we were sympathetic to producers' problems," a European delegate says. "Now we enter negotiations to obtain the best possible deal for ourselves."

Commodity pacts generally rely on quotas and buffer stocks, or common inventories, to keep prices in an agreed range. The intent is to assure stable supplies and output, and an orderly market for producers and consumers alike.

When a commodity's price falls below a specified level, the accord's representatives typically buy it on the market to force quotas back up. When prices surge, the council sells surpluses from its stockpile. Producers can also agree to restrict exports when the market is weak and to suspend quotas when prices are high.

[B] In practice, though, producing members of several pacts have ignored quotas and stepped up output, even at low prices, because they need foreign currency to repay international loans.

[C] Actions of non-member producers also put strain on cartels. While the sugar pact imposed strict export quotas on its producing nations, the Common Market, a major producer, didn't belong to the world

organization. **Huge amounts of Common Market sugar poured into the international market, undermining prices.**

[D] The high prices maintained by the tin pact discouraged consumption, and other metals such as aluminum became popular. Meanwhile Brazil, a tin producer that wasn't a member of the commodity pact, flooded the market, dealers say.

The cocoa pact, which failed dismally to support prices a few years ago, is being tested again this year after a major hitch was straightened out. The buffer-stock manager at the International Cocoa Organization now can buy from producers that aren't members, such as Malaysia. Last month the manager kept prices from falling by purchasing cocoa both from member and non-member countries, although one analyst says the manager isn't buying very aggressively.

Mr. Fish warns that if cocoa surpluses continue to swamp the market, the buffer stock manager will soon exhaust his $250 million purchase budget. Just such a drain helped stymie previous price-support efforts. When prices fell in 1984, the market anticipated the moves by the buffer stock manager and waited them out.

The rubber pact is working best because it is elastic, says a delegate to several commodity organizations. Price ranges at which the buffer-stock manager trades are adjusted to reflect market forces. Export quotas aren't used.

Some commodity agreements have been undermined when threats by some producers to form their own cartels antagonized consumer members. In the tin organization, Malaysia, Indonesia and Thailand plied a separate course, and Latin American coffee producers raised the specter of their own coffee group.

Indonesia, the world's third-largest coffee producer, has said it will seek more support in the ICO from Asian-Pacific nations. Indonesia, the Phillippines, Thailand and Singapore are members of the Asean coffee club, formed in 1980. Asean—the Association of Southeast Asian Nations—also includes Malaysia and Brunei.

Indonesia and seven other coffee producers have said demands by Brazil and 23 other producers to maintain the traditional ICO quotas are unrealistic. Quotas were suspended in February 1986 when prices soared to more than $2 a pound because of drought damage to the crop in Brazil, the world's largest producer with an ICO quota of 30% of the market. Coffee stood at $1.12 a pound Friday.

Market forces, too, have militated against commodity pacts. Supplies of raw materials surged in the 1980s as Third World nations overproduced, spurred by the price gains of the 1970s.

Meanwhile agricultural subsidies in the Common Market, the U.S. and elsewhere accentuated the commodities glut that led to the inevitable failure of the pacts, says John Calverly, an economist at American Express Bank.

On the other hand, when demand for sugar surged in 1980, prices more than doubled despite the stabilization efforts of the international organization.

In recent years consuming nations have lost enthusiasm for the idea of commodity price and production stabilization. Although they were receptive in the 1970s when they wanted to curb rapidly climbing prices, analysts say, the subsequent commodities slump has helped curb runaway inflation in major consuming countries.

[E] Still, self-interest may encourage some consuming nations to stick with commodity pacts. Latin American countries are having trouble repaying bank loans, and in one analyst's view that is a big incentive for consuming countries to prop prices for coffee and cocoa. ∎

QUESTIONS

1. Passages A to D illustrate four serious problems faced by would-be cartels. What are these problems?
2. Passages B and E concern efforts by developing countries to repay international loans. But the passages appear to be contradictory: passage B indicates that extra revenue for debt payments comes from output expansion while passage E indicates that the extra revenue comes from output contraction.

   a. Who faces a higher elasticity of demand for output, an individual cartel member or the entire cartel as a group? Explain briefly.
   b. Based on your answer to part **a,** how, if at all, can passages B and E both make sense?

This article documents the fact that financial aid officials from twenty-three select Eastern colleges have been meeting privately for years to make sure that a student seeking financial aid was offered roughly the same amount by each school. It also indicates some of the problems this "cartel" is experiencing, problems that are typical of those that almost all successful cartels must overcome. The last two questions examine financial aid policies as an example of price discrimination.

23 Colleges in East Adjust Aid to Avert Bidding for Students

By FOX BUTTERFIELD

WELLESLEY, Mass., April 15—For two decades officials representing a group of select Eastern colleges have met privately to insure that a student seeking financial aid was offered roughly the same amount by each school.

"Some people tease us and say it's price fixing, but it's not," said Amy Nychis, director of financial aid at Wellesley, where officials of 23 schools met last week." The basic purpose is to give students and their parents the freedom of choice to go to the school they really want and not to pick because one school offers them more aid than another."

Another purpose, some college officials acknowledge, is to help the schools stretch their financial aid budgets and avoid possible bidding wars over the most attractive students.

In some cases college officials may raise or lower their financial aid offers to a student after seeing what other schools have offered.

The meetings, which are not widely known about by students and parents, grew out of the shift in the late 1950's and early 1960's from scholarships based on academic or athletic ability toward aid based entirely on need.

But some officials at this year's meeting were surprised when two of the participating schools, Smith and Mount Holyoke, disclosed that they were introducing a new program to attract top students by offering cash grants regardless of need.

Although administrators at Smith and Mount Holyoke insisted the new awards were not merit aid be-cause the amounts were relatively small, only $300 or $400 apiece, officials at several schools said they were concerned that the action might put pressure on other colleges to offer their own financial inducements as the number of college-age students declines.

[A] "I think all of us would prefer Smith and Mount Holyoke not do it," a financial aid officer at another small New England college said. "It's a crack in the dike. The question arises, if they don't get the students with that amount of money, how much more will they offer, and won't other schools follow?"

Several colleges outside the 23-member group, including Northwestern and Duke, have recently begun offering some merit-based scholarships to attract top students as part of what some university officials said might be the beginning of a national trend.

Discrepancies Resolved

The annual meeting at Wellesley came after the colleges made their final selection of high school seniors and a week before today's mailing of acceptance notices to students.

The participating colleges were the eight members of the Ivy League (Brown, Columbia, Cornell, Dartmouth, Harvard, the University of Pennsylvania, Princeton and Yale), Barnard, Bryn Mawr, Mount Holyoke, Smith, Vassar and Wellesley, the Massachusetts Institute of Technology, and a group called the Pentagonials, consisting of Amherst, Williams, Wesleyan, Bowdoin, Colby, Tufts, Middlebury and Trinity.

Seamus Malin, director of financial aid at Harvard, said that in most cases the school officials were "fairly much in agreement" on how much aid a student would need and how much the parents should contribute.

But in about a third of the cases there are "wide discrepancies," which Mr. Malin described as $2,000 to $3,000. That, he noted, is still a small amount of the total cost of a year's education at an Ivy League school, which will range up from the $13,200 charged at Cornell this year, with all fees included.

It is these larger variations in proposed aid that the officials try to resolve in their annual conferences by either raising or lowering their offers to students.

'Nothing Sneaky Going On'

There is no rule requiring the schools to agree on the amount of parental contribution for a student who has been accepted at several colleges, Mr. Malin explained, but the officers generally narrow their differences to within $100 or so.

"It is a delicate issue in a sense," he conceded. "But there is nothing sneaky going on. It is not the Ivies getting together and dividing the talent."

School officials are normally close in their assessments of each student's needs, Mr. Malin said, because they work with standardized information and methods.

Every applicant for financial aid must first submit a form disclosing his parents' income and assets to the College Scholarship Service in Princeton, N.J., a division of the Educational Testing Service. The service analyzes this form by computer and sends the results to each school to which the student has applied.

The colleges then make their own analyses, Mr. Malin said, and it is at this stage that the variations in aid arise. A particular school may request more data from the parents, or an applicant may have a brother or sister at one of the colleges, which provides that school with additional financial information.

'Bidding' on Aid Denied

Financial aid officers at several of the colleges strongly denied that any member of their group would increase an aid offer after the meeting to entice a student coveted by the school, such as a bright young scientist or football player.

"There is a lot of pressure not to do that," said Jacqueline Foster, director of the undergraduate financial aid office at Yale. She added that "it would get back to you very quickly" because the parents might go to another college to see if they could get a higher offer there, too.

Nevertheless, an official at Brown said, some colleges might try to make their offer more attractive by raising the amount of grant assistance. Each aid package is made up of three parts: a grant, a loan and self-help work provided by the school.

More controversial are the new grants based on a student's ability rather than need. A spokesman for Smith, Ann Shanahan, said the school had decided to award 36 achievement awards of $300 each to "the students we most want to have come to Smith."

"We don't think of them as merit aid because the amounts are so small," she said, adding that the money for the grants came from special funds designated by the administration and not out of regular aid allocations.

Pat Waters, director of financial aid at Mount Holyoke, said her school would provide 30 students with grants of $400 each regardless of financial need. She described them as "prizes" rather than aid, because, she said, "The amount isn't large enough to make anyone change their mind." ■

QUESTIONS

1. A group of twenty-three select Eastern colleges have met privately to insure that a student seeking financial aid was offered roughly the same amount by each school in the group. What obstacles must be overcome by any group of sellers attempting to "collude" and "fix" prices? Use the article for ideas in this regard.

2. Which of the obstacles in question 1 are causing difficulty for this specific group of sellers? Explain.

3. Consider the last two paragraphs of the article:
   a. Do you agree with Pat Waters from Mount Holyoke that "the amount isn't large enough to make anyone change their mind"? If you disagree, why? If you agree, what justification would you give for Mount Holyoke's providing such prizes?
   b. Does the financial aid officer quoted in passage A agree with Pat Waters? Explain briefly.

4. Do you think providing differing amounts of financial aid to different students is a form of "price discrimination"? Explain.

5. Is the common practice of giving more scholarship aid to "needier" students consistent with profit maximization? What about "achievement awards" of the type given by Smith and Mount Holyoke? Explain your answers.

This information from an antitrust suit brought against Alcoa some time ago is meant to illustrate "price leadership" as one way in which price collusion occurred in the aluminum industry. Note that Alcoa is not always the "leader" at this stage in the industry's history, although it apparently was almost always the leader in the 1940s. Note also that the August 4, 1952, move was a result of government price controls.

Timing of Changes in Prices of 99% Plus Primary Aluminum Ingot

	Three Leading Companies, 1950–1956		
Price	Alcoa	Reynolds Metals	Kaiser
$.175	May 22, 1950	May 23, 1950	May 25, 1950
.190	Sept. 25, 1950	Sept. 29, 1950	Sept. 28, 1950
.200	Aug. 4, 1952	Aug. 4, 1952	Aug. 4, 1952
.205	Jan. 23, 1953	Jan. 23, 1953	Jan. 22, 1953
.215	July 15, 1953	July 20, 1953	July 20, 1953
.222	Aug. 5, 1954	Aug. 6, 1954	Aug. 6, 1954
.232	Jan. 13, 1955	Jan. 10, 1955	Jan. 12, 1955
.244	Aug. 1, 1955	Aug. 6, 1955	Aug. 2, 1955
.259	Mar. 29, 1956	Mar. 27, 1956	Mar. 26, 1956

Source: United States v. Aluminum Company of America, 153 F. Supp. 151.

QUESTIONS

1. Do you think it is just coincidence that once one major aluminum producer raised its price, the other two followed suit? Why or why not?

2. Does your answer to question 1 imply anything about the market structure of this industry?

This article reports an accusation of predatory pricing between two small copying firms in Harvard Square in the mid-1970s and deals with the issues of predatory pricing and barriers to entry. The questions accompanying the article address the credibility of predation as a motive and probe alternative explanations for what might have been occurring instead.

Copy Cat Service Tells 'Other Side' of Pricing Battle

By DAVID B. HILDER

James Jacobs, owner of the Copy Cat Xerox copying service in the J. August clothing store, yesterday fired another salvo in the Mass Ave Xerox copying price war.

Jacobs posted two of his employees outside J. August and Gnomon Copy on Mass Ave to distribute leaflets announcing that Copy Cat's price of two cents per copy will be guaranteed until December 31.

The two-cents-per-copy price may be extended beyond December 31, Jacobs said yesterday, but added that he may increase the price after that date if the Xerox Corporation increases the prices of supplies.

Jacob's leaflet carried the announcement of the price guarantee on one side and a copy of a leaflet that Gnomon Copy distributed last week on the other side, along with a handwritten statement that Copy Cat "will not be intimidated to raise prices to Gnomon levels."

The leaflet that Gnomon distributed last week alleged that Copy Cat was selling copies at a price below cost, so as to cut out all competition and ultimately raise its prices.

Jacobs said yesterday that his leaflet "told both sides of the story."

Since Copy Cat lowered its price and the leafletting barrages began last week, business has increased for both the copying service and the J. August store, Jacobs said yesterday.

John Sytek, vice president of Gnomon Copy, said last night Gnomon will continue to match J. August's price on loose original copy orders until December 31, but added he is not sure what Gnomon's pricing policy would be after that date. ■

QUESTIONS

1. Gnomon has accused Copy Cat of what type of conduct?
2. What, if any, significant barriers to entry do you think might exist in the local photocopy market?
3. Given your answers to questions 1 and 2, do you agree with Gnomon? Why or why not?
4. What other rationale can you think of for the Xerox pricing policy used by Copy Cat (J. August)? *Hint:* Does the fact that photocopying is only one of its activities give you any ideas?

From *The Harvard Crimson,* October 30, 1975. Reprinted by permission.

This article provides an excellent opportunity to apply and contrast the models of perfect competition and monopoly. It describes the attempts by major cities to "deregulate" the taxicab industry by getting rid of restrictions on entry and price. The deregulation described here parallels the more familiar cases of airline and trucking deregulation.

The Drive Is on to Deregulate Taxicabs

Help may be on the way for millions of Americans across the country trying in vain to hail a cab during rush hour. The trend toward deregulation, which started five years ago on the West Coast, has just been given a boost from the Federal Trade Commission. The FTC is charging that taxi regulation by Minneapolis and New Orleans amounts to illegal collusion. Although that charge has met resistance in Congress, deregulation seems unstoppable. Kansas City has just taken steps to expand the number of its cabs, and Houston and Chicago are considering opening up entry, joining the list of 24 cities that have begun to deregulate.

For more than 50 years regulations limiting the number of cabs have kept the supply artificially low. Cities have also fixed fares, raising them about in line with inflation but not enough to keep the $3.4 billion industry healthy. Service has declined along with ridership. Gorman Gilbert, a transportation expert at the University of North Carolina, figures ridership fell 25% from 1973 to 1981, as taxis lost out to private autos, rental cars, and even mass transit.

"The industry is in bad shape," says Roger F. Teal of the University of California at Irvine. "The market is being eroded, and the industry has a smaller and smaller patronage base." Many economists argue that deregulation will revitalize it.

'Formerly Stodgy'

The number of cabs operating in cities that have opened entry has greatly increased. In San Diego, three years after deregulation, taxi permits rose 84%, from 409 to 752. The number of cab companies nearly tripled, and the share of permits held by the largest company fell from 68% to 37%. In Seattle, there were 25% more cabs two years after controls were lifted.

Service also appears to have improved. Studies done for the Transportation Dept. reveal that the percentage of riders who rate the San Diego taxi system favorably went from 75% before deregulation to 82% the year after. In Seattle, where comparative surveys were not available, Transportation found that "overwhelming majorities of both residents and visitors gave positive ratings" to taxi service after deregulation.

Competition is also forcing taxi companies to become more efficient and innovative. "Some formerly very stodgy taxicab companies are doing some exciting things," says Robert W. Poole Jr., president of Reason Foundation, which tracks deregulation. The City of Phoenix contracts with taxi companies to supply public transportation on Sunday, when no buses run. In San Diego, the number of companies providing jitney services—carrying riders on fixed routes—nearly doubled in the three years following deregulation. In Seattle and Phoenix, the radio-equipped fleet cabs virtually abandoned the airports to nonradio cabs, which had flocked to them. Instead, they concentrate on radio calls, making more taxicabs available to city residents.

In Raleigh, N.C., which has had an open taxi industry for years, Raleigh Transportation Services developed a computer system that searches out its 30 cabs to find the one nearest a specific address. President William W. Williams hopes to put a dashboard terminal in each cab. His investment contradicts opponents' claims that investment occurs only if taxis are regulated.

So far, fares have not declined after deregulation. But in part that is because they were kept too low for so long, economists maintain. Many deregulated companies are raising prices to catch up. Yet in real terms—adjusted for inflation—they have fallen. Pat M. Gelb, an analyst with De Leuw, Cather & Co. in San Francisco, says that the average taxi fare in San Diego was 28% higher three years after deregulation. This increase was less than the 39% rise in the consumer price index and the 42% national average rise in fares during that period.

Richard O. Zerbe Jr. of the University of Washington compared taxi price increases in the two-and-a-half years after Seattle's deregulation with the pace of price increases during the previous 12 years. Before deregulation, fares averaged 99% of the national CPI and only 92% afterwards.

[A] Consumer information about fares has been the biggest issue surrounding deregulation. Zerbe found that while airport and cruising cab fares went up 25% and 30%, respectively, fares for radio calls went up only 6%. The radio market, he notes, permits customers to shop around for better prices. But this is not the case at airports: Cab drivers there could often gouge unsuspecting travelers. Airports took on what the University of California's Teal called a "Turkish bazaar atmosphere." The confusion so embarrassed city officials in Seattle and Phoenix that they instituted some controls at the airports. Atlanta, which has had open entry since 1965, put controls back on in 1981 after business leaders worried about the city's image. In 1983 San Diego put a one-year moratorium on new permits.

Such problems have bolstered opposition to deregulation. Taxi owners are among the fiercest opponents. "The current cabs would be devastated," says Joseph M. Chernow, president of Yellow Cab Co. in Houston. In March, several hundred San Francisco cab drivers circled City Hall, blasting their horns, trying to dissuade Mayor Dianne Feinstein from increasing the city's 711 cab permits to 1,000 by 1986. So far, only 50 permits have been added.

Gypsies and Bandits

Supporters of deregulation admit that problems may be inevitable at first. "People arrived off the plane with no earthly idea that the city had deregulated," says Otto A. Davis, an economist at Carnegie-Mellon University. "Given our tradition of fixed fares, there's no reason to expect deregulation to have worked out." But better publicity and better design of airport taxi lines could correct the problem, proponents contend.

Some even approve of partial regulation. Says economist John R. Meyer of Harvard: "It would be hard to argue that opening up entry is not helpful to the consumer. But perhaps you need minor controls to correct the information problems."

[B] What is not needed, they argue, is the suffocating regulation of the past. That has led to high prices for the right to operate a cab. In Boston, which allows no more cabs than it did in 1930, a taxi license costs about $33,000. In New York City, the going price is $63,000 to $70,000. Deregulation would reduce the value of taxi medallions and thus would almost certainly be challenged as government confiscation of property. How the courts would rule is an "open issue," says Robert Mackasek, Deputy Commissioner of the New York City Taxi & Limousine Commission.

Squeezed out by high medallion prices, many taxi operators exist outside the law. Known as "gypsies," "bandits," and "hacks," they serve mostly ghetto neighborhoods. Davis of Carnegie-Mellon found nearly twice as many illegal cabs in Pittsburgh as legal ones. New York City has an estimated 20,000 to 40,000 gypsies, compared with 12,000 licensed cabs.

These unofficial taxis help meet the demand for cab service, but many lack adequate insurance and are costly to police. Deregulation could reduce the problem of gypsies, as well as improve service for cab riders everywhere. ∎

QUESTIONS

1. What form did the regulation of the taxicab industry take before the "trend toward deregulation"?

2. If you had been asked to predict (using economic theory) the effects of "deregulation" on price and output, what predictions would you have made?

3. Indicate any evidence presented in this article that seems consistent with your predictions above. Indicate any that seems inconsistent.

4. Consider passage B:
   a. With taxi deregulation, how much do you think taxi medallions will be worth? Why?
   b. Based on your answer to part a, what does taxi regulation do that makes taxi medallions worth so much? Explain.

   c. Is the effect of regulation discussed in part b in the public interest? Why or why not?

5. Consider passage A:
   a. What accounts for the difference in fares in the airport and cruising cabs market on the one hand and in the radio call market on the other?
   b. Do you think this difference may be an obstacle to complete deregulation? Why or why not?

6. Who do you think would be the major beneficiaries of the deregulation of the taxicab industry? Who would be worse off?

In this article, FTC Chairman James Miller cites many examples of anticompetitive conduct by health-care professionals. The article illustrates how competition makes as much economic sense for professional services as it does for other, less "glamorous" goods and services.

Mr. Miller of the FTC Takes on the Doctors

By MARGARET GARRARD WARNER

WASHINGTON—One year ago, James Miller III was battling regulation as head of President Reagan's regulatory-reform task force. Newspapers described him as "deregulation czar" so often, says the Georgia-born economist, that "some folks figured it was part of my name."

So when Mr. Miller became Federal Trade Commission Chairman last October, the betting was that he'd rein in the controversial agency whenever and wherever he could. And he is trimming the FTC's sails. But one of the fiercest fights he's gotten into has been to maintain the agency's jurisdiction over the economy's fastest growing sector, professional services.

Mr. Miller is up against a well-financed lobbying campaign led by doctors, dentists and optometrists. They are trying to convince Congress that more than a dozen state-licensed professions and their trade associations should be made exempt from FTC scrutiny or prosecution. Operating under the banner of deregulation, the doctors are making significant headway in the Senate and House.

The 40-year-old Mr. Miller, a former economics professor and American Enterprise Institute scholar with a passionate belief in the free market, charges that the doctors are distorting the basic premise of deregulation to exploit its political appeal. A true deregulator believes in unfettered markets, Mr. Miller maintains, "and the fact is that many of these markets are not free, when professionals and their trade associations can join in cartel-like activities that drive up prices, inhibit competition and stifle innovation."

But the new FTC chief, who calls the doctors' proposal "old-fashioned protectionism," is discovering that their political clout can't be so easily dismissed. To his dismay, a number of Republicans who espouse free-market principles have sided with the doctors. In a recent interview, Mr. Miller discussed the doctors' arguments from a free-marketer's perspective.

In answer to the argument that the FTC is trying to shut down legitimate professional self-regulation that maintains the quality of health care, Mr. Miller says: "That's hogwash. The doctors are right about one thing—the FTC doesn't have the expertise to judge their work. I wouldn't know poison ivy from impetigo, and I don't have any interest in being in the position of deciding who does.

"On the other hand, we do have people at this agency with expertise in generic problems associated with business. Price-fixing, boycotts or fraud can crop up in the business of providing medicine as easily as they can in any other business. The incentive is always there. And in the case of health care professionals, anticompetitive business practices sometimes have the weight of tradition behind them. We've had to challenge a local medical society for denying local hospital privileges to physicians who worked for the HMOs (prepaid medical-care plans). We've had to challenge a group of doctors for threatening to boycott their small town's only hospital emergency room if the hospital recruited any more doctors to work there.

"These activities have little or nothing to do with the quality of medical care that's offered. They're commercial activities, good old-fashioned business practices that happen to violate the antitrust laws. I don't think they should be overlooked simply because individuals with advanced degrees are engaging in them."

Mr. Miller says the argument that FTC involvement amounts to usurping states' rights, since the states license these professions, is "another red herring. Don't confuse the licensing of professionals—which is intended to maintain certain qualifications and standards—with regulating professionals' overall business conduct.

"All of the antitrust cases we've brought against professionals have challenged *private* restraints, not practices established and actively supervised. And I'll accept legislation barring us outright from ever challenging a state in antitrust matters.

[A] **"But in our other incarnation—protecting consumers against unfairness and deception—we did promulgate one industrywide rule that overturned some state laws. That was our eyeglass rule." That rule threw out professional and state bans against advertising eyeglass and contact lens prices. "In three years," says Mr. Miller, "the average price of a pair of soft contact lenses dropped by about $100 in constant dollars, thanks to the new competitive environment stimulated by price advertising.**

"In cases like this, I feel that the FTC, the feds, have a proper role in making sure that the market works in a way that gives consumers the opportunity to make choices. It's a matter of finding the balance between federalism on the one hand and devotion to economic efficiency and free markets on the other."

Mr. Miller vigorously disputes the doctors' contention that their proposal is consistent with the administration's deregulatory efforts.

"Look, I'm an economist by trade. I've been involved in a couple of successful deregulation projects like trucking and airlines, and I think I know what deregulation looks like," he says. "Believe me, this ain't the animal.

"All you have to do is look at the professions to see that many of these markets are not free. They're not unregulated. They are fettered, in fact, by their own members.

"And look at the results. In 1980, this country spent $247 billion for health care, nearly 10% of our gross national product. Thirty years ago it was a little more than 4%. Yet we recently found evidence that doctors and dentists in several states conspired to undermine cost-containment programs that were developed by insurance companies, corporation managers and labor unions.

"And what about innovation? In a *free* market you'd see innovation in how services are delivered. Yet in medical care, innovation has been awfully slow in coming. And why? Well, the AMA (American Medical Association) codes, which we challenged, barred doctors from working for low-cost health-maintenance plans, for one. And in Kentucky, we found a group of doctors wanting to offer a house-call service were barred from publicizing that fact by the AMA's guidelines.

"What the FTC represents," Mr. Miller declares, "is not a vehicle to add government regulation, but a force to root out regulation of the self-imposed sort. That's how you restore a truly free market."

Mr. Miller believes that the doctors' campaign is making gains in Congress nonetheless because "they have a damaging argument . . . that has nothing to do with this issue. It's the argument that the Federal Trade Commission is a bunch of zealots who won't treat you fairly, an agency that's arrogant and eager to jerk people around."

The willingness of many lawmakers to believe such criticisms today frustrates the agency's new chief. "When I started last year," he says, "I thought that when Miller and his new team of people came over here, there would be a perception on the Hill that a different day had dawned, and debate on an issue involving this agency wouldn't be colored by the hostility of what went before. . . . Naive, I guess, very naive."

Mr. Miller doesn't blame lavish contributions for turning lawmakers' heads on this issue, as many critics do. But he does fault legislators, including Republican ones, for falling for what he regards as a none-too-subtle manipulation of political labels. "You have a Republican congressman or senator who's very oriented to states' rights and someone comes in to him and says, 'The FTC is trying to overrule the states,'" Mr. Miller says, "and this legislator's gut reaction is, 'By God, we've got to stop the FTC from doing that.'"

"The debate seems to have come down to either a wholesale examption for professionals, or no change at all," he says. "It's frustrating to me, because I'm in the middle ground. I'm advocating specific changes in our statutory authority to make sure the rules are clear and fair, so we don't have situations that give rise to what I think are some legitimate gripes the professionals have about their past treatment by this agency. But my position is, once that's done, then the rules should be applied equally to everybody." ∎

QUESTIONS

1. Professional associations have repeatedly attempted to gain an exemption from U.S. antitrust laws. Both of the following arguments have reached the Supreme Court. Briefly decide whether you agree or disagree with each of the following, and use evidence from the article to support your position:

    a. "Competition is inconsistent with the

practice of a profession because enhancing profit is not the goal of professional activities; the goal is to provide services necessary to the community." (Goldfarb v. Virginia State Bar [1975])

b. Restricting price competition for professional services should not be considered an antitrust violation. For professional services, what matters is quality, not price. (National Society of Professional Engineers v. U.S. [1978])

2. Consider passage A: Can Mr. Miller be right? Since advertising raises costs, how can it result in lower prices?

> The incorporation of rent-seeking activities into monopoly theory significantly alters the conventional analysis of the welfare costs of monopoly. This article reports on beer wholesalers in California who attempt to acquire legislative approval for exclusive territorial franchises (common in other states). Questions accompanying the article deal with the feedback between monopoly profits and rent-seeking activities.

Beer Wholesalers Push for Monopoly

By LEO C. WOLINSKY

SACRAMENTO—In theory at least, the network of businesses that make up California's beer distribution system should be a textbook example of free competition.

Brewers large and small sell the product under a variety of brand names. An estimated 200 independent wholesalers distribute it to 60,000 retail stores and saloons throughout California. They, in turn, vie for a share of the beer-drinking public. The system has worked well, the industry contends, providing Californians with beer prices that are among the lowest in the nation.

A key segment of the industry—the middlemen who buy the beer from the brewers and deliver it to the retail market—is pushing legislation that would, however, fundamentally alter the equation by granting individual wholesalers monopoly territories and forbidding retailers from buying from anyone else.

Consumer groups and retailers, who have launched a heavy lobbying effort to defeat the bill, say the wholesalers' intent is to establish control over the state's beer distribution network, stymieing the ability of stores to shop for bargains and eventually raising beer prices for consumers.

"This is an outright power grab for a monopoly." said Walter Zelman, executive director of California Common Cause. "They want any store in any area to be told that 'This is it; you buy from me or you don't sell at all.'"

The wholesalers, among the top contributors to political campaigns in California, acknowledge that they have seized control of 90% of beer sales in the state by carving out exclusive territories for themselves. Their agreements, however, do not have the force of law.

Their continuing complaint is with the remaining 10% of the market, in which a few distributors still compete with each other and big chain stores are able to shop around for the best deals or buy direct from the brewers.

Assemblyman Jim Costa (D-Fresno), who is carrying the bill for the wholesalers, maintains that "the consumer effects of the bill are positive and that prices will remain stable." The aim of the measure, he said, is to help small stores and bars that might not be served if the big chains have their way and the current distribution system falters.

"I'm talking about mom-and-pop grocery stores and the individual neighborhood pubs," Costa said. "This will ensure their livelihood is protected."

Susan Romeo, a public relations executive hired to plead the case of the wholesalers, added, "I could see where the entire industry could be threatened, because there would no longer be any use for wholesalers."

At least 28 states have adopted similar legislation, although Congress has repeatedly rejected efforts to allow monopoly territories nationwide.

The battle pits several powerful special interests against each other, but the stakes are equally high for consumers. According to industry figures, Californians drink nearly 640 million gallons of beer a year, an average of 24 gallons a person, pushing annual sales to $4 billion statewide. Beer wholesalers employ an estimated 10,000 workers.

The heavily lobbied legislation passed its first hurdle Tuesday night, when the Assembly Governmental Organization Committee approved the measure on a bipartisan 10–3 vote after more than an hour of sometimes angry testimony. Scores of lobbyists and industry representatives were on hand to witness the victory.

Although the committee's swift approval underscored the political clout of the beer wholesalers, its vote may not be a true test of the measure's viability.

The committee, which has jurisdiction over most alcohol-related bills, has a reputation favored by the alcoholic beverage industry. The beer distributors gave more than $370,000 to legislative and statewide political campaigns over the last two years, enough to rank them eighth among contributors. More than $43,000 of that was specifically targeted for members of the Governmental Operations Committee. Retailers also contribute, but far less—about one-fourth as much in the last two years.

The wholesalers, by contrast, have far less clout in the Assembly Ways and Means Committee, where the bill goes next. Its members hear legislation with a potential financial impact, diluting the influence of any single special-interest group.

A bill almost identical to the current beer measure stalled in Ways and Means two years ago amid public controversy. This year's version of the beer bill, however, bears striking resemblance to a measure approved by the Legislature in 1985 that would have created monopoly territories for wholesalers of fine wines. That legislation, intended to kill a flourishing market in cheap imports of prestige French champagne, was vetoed by Gov. George Deukmejian as anti-competitive.

This year's beer bill would carve the state into a number of distribution territories and grant exclusive rights to individual wholesalers to operate within those areas. Retailers would be barred from shopping different wholesalers for the best price or from purchasing from any source outside their designated territory.

Particularly worrisome to chain stores is a prohibition on transferring beer from one store to another or even storing beer at a central warehouse.

"Grocers like myself would be forced to accept whatever price a wholesaler wants for beer," complained Manuel Campos, who owns four grocery stores in Northern California. "As a result, beer prices for my customers will increase. . . . I think all businessmen and women would love the luxury of being the only seller of a product in a defined territory, but that isn't fair to consumers."

[A] Paul DeNio, lobbyist for the wholesalers, countered that the beer distributors "have a major investment" in their businesses and need protection of law so they can remain profitable and continue to serve small grocery stores and bars that otherwise might have difficulty finding anyone to sell to them.

"That's where we create competition," DeNio said.

Costa, the bill's author, added that wholesalers perform other important functions, such as restocking shelves and rotating stock so that stale beer is not sold. And he indicated that the law could help discourage lawsuits between wholesalers and breweries over contractual arrangements.

Don Beaver, lobbyist, for the California Retailers Assn., called those arguments "a whole bunch of senseless baloney," adding, "This is all a smoke screen, and the real issue is they want exclusive territories. . . . It's very anti-consumer and anti-competitive and anti-everything else."

The major question looming over the debate is how much, if at all, beer prices would rise should this bill pass.

Although wholesalers control about 90% of the beer market through exclusive contracts arranged with brewers, prices average about $2.09 for a six-pack, among the lowest in the nation. That would appear to weaken opponents' arguments that exclusive territories automatically drive prices up.

Retailers and consumer advocates insist that prices have stayed low only because of the 10% of the business that remains competitive. Take that away, they say, and there is no telling what might happen.

Their argument is bolstered by a major study last year by the legislative analyst's office that concluded that a bill like the current one would "place upward pressures on the prices" and would leave "California beer consumers as a whole . . . worse off than they would be without such a bill."

Consumer groups, meanwhile, said that if necessary they will take their fight to communities, informing voters that their representatives are about to help raise prices on a favorite beverage, just before summer's heavy beer-drinking season.

Harry Snyder, West Coast director of Consumers Union, warned members of the Governmental Organizations Committee during its hearing Tuesday night that the bill will hurt "everyone in your district that does not run or work for a beer wholesaler. . . . This is probably the most embarrassing bill this committee will see this year." ■

QUESTIONS

1. Use a supply and demand diagram to contrast a competitive and a monopoly equilibrium in the wholesale market for beer. Assume that the wholesale cost of beer is constant.
2. Indicate in your diagram the most that beer wholesalers would spend in lobbying for a monopoly.
3. Consider a successful lobbying effort:
   a. Indicate in your diagram the conventional social welfare loss associated with the beer distribution monopoly.
   b. Suppose the distributors' lobbying expenses correspond to real social costs such as the salaries of lobbyists and the campaign expenses of legislators who support the beer wholesalers. What area in your diagram corresponds to the possible additional social welfare loss of the monopoly?
4. Consider passage A: Can you think of other industries that might make use of a similar argument for monopoly protection? Explain briefly.

This article on the salary arbitration award of baseball pitcher Fernando Valenzuela demonstrates that Valenzuela's agent implicitly relied on the concept of marginal revenue product to win the case. Information from the article is useful for computing a quantitative estimate of Valenzuela's marginal revenue product and for assessing whether Valenzuela was "worth" his million-dollar salary.

Fernando Hits Jackpot for Million

By MARK HEISLER

VERO BEACH, Fla.—In the time it took arbitrator Tom Roberts to place a call from his home in Rolling Hills Estates to the Major League Players Assn. in New York City, 22-year-old Fernando Valenzuela became the highest-paid Dodger, the highest-paid third-year player in baseball history and the first man ever to be awarded $1 million in arbitration.

Roberts decided Saturday for Valenzuela and against the Dodgers, who had submitted a $750,000 offer.

That ended the Dodgers' arbitration win streak at three and enabled Valenzuela's lawyer, Dick Moss, 3–1 in arbitrations, to tie Bob Walker, the heretofore undefeated Dodger counsel, who is now 3–1 himself.

"I would like to congratulate Tony DeMarco and Dick Moss for what must have been a very impressive case," said Dodger owner Peter O'Malley here Saturday night.

"We gave the arbitrators four tough cases (the team beat Pedro Guerrero, Steve Howe and Mike Scioscia). We thought they were very fair, very professional. We appreciate the job the arbitrators did."

This is how impressive Valenzuela's case was: It included endorsements from Al Campanis and Tom Lasorda, who are the Dodger executive vice president for personnel and the Dodger manager, respectively.

This was done in a 3½-minute videotape, accepted by Roberts during the Friday hearing only after Walker objected and Moss counterobjected for close to half an hour.

The tape included Lasorda, being interviewed in 1981, Valenzuela's rookie year, at the height of Fernandomania. On the tape, Lasorda says things like:

"Everywhere we go the fans are clamoring for Fernando."

And:

"Fernando is a player who comes along once in a lifetime."

And:

"I'm the luckiest manager in the world."

Campanis was interviewed, also in 1981, standing on an empty baseball diamond. A friend of Valenzuela's, who saw the tape, insists Campanis even had tears in his eyes. Campanis says something like:

"Mr. Walter O'Malley must be looking down and smiling. When we moved to Los Angeles, he asked me, 'Al, do you think we can find a good Mexican player?' Fernando is the answer to all our dreams and prayers. We're so lucky."

Years later, the Dodgers have a good Mexican player, if an expensive one. If Mr. Peter O'Malley was gracious enough Saturday, he did, however, manage to stop short of endorsing Roberts' decision.

"I assume you know how many pitchers there are making $1 million a year," O'Malley said. "Now there are two." (Nolan Ryan is the other.)

In the homes of Valenzuela, DeMarco and Moss, in Bunker Hill, Hollywood and Pacific Palisades, respectively, jubilation reigned.

DeMarco, who was criticized to the point of being personally whipsawed in last spring's holdout, expressed his "happiness and relief." Fernando, he said, was home, feeling "happy and calm."

The debate in the hearing went this way: On behalf of the Dodgers, Walker, as is his custom, argued that Valenzuela should be compensated according to his experience. The contract the team was offering was higher than any third-year man had ever received (Rickey Henderson had the old record, $535,000).

Among left-handed pitchers, it was exceeded only by Steve Carlton's $800,000.

Moss argued that Valenzuela's performance over two seasons placed him with the game's best pitchers, and that Valenzuela also enjoyed an extraordinary appeal. Moss introduced exhibits demonstrating that Carlton, for example, had drawn a few more fans than the Phillies' average in 1981, but no more in 1982.

No other starting pitcher in the major leagues makes a difference in attendance, according to Moss (Moss, it should be noted, also represents Ryan.)

[A] "We did what I thought was a sophisticated breakdown of Dodger attendance," Moss said Saturday night. "It shows that Fernando produces about 15,000 people when he pitches at home on a weekday.

"The Dodgers always sell out weekends and they sell out on their promotion days. But for weekday, non-promotion nights, there was an extra difference between Valenzuela and the other pitchers.

"The bottom line was that when Fernando Valenzuela pitches, it's a promotion."

Valenzuela is now expected to report in a week to start working on his second million. O'Malley, asked if Saturday's decision was going to change anything, maybe push the team more toward a long-term contract, said he didn't think so.

"Maybe we'll let salary discussions cool off for a while," O'Malley said. " . . . We think well of him (Valenzuela). We think he's an outstanding pitcher. If he continues that performance, he'll be paid handsomely. . . .

"I don't think anybody knows where it (salaries) can go. It's blue sky." Arbitrators don't discuss their cases, and Roberts held to that Saturday, complimenting both sides, but refusing to say how he arrived at his decision.

"I've never seen as much interest in a case," he said. "Both cases were argued with great skill. It was a very difficult decision."

According to a friend of Valenzuela, Roberts had indicated to someone at the Players Assn. office that the decision had not been difficult. Roberts suggested that it had been.

"I put in a lot of work, a lot of hours," he said. ∎

QUESTIONS

1. A typical starting pitcher makes about twelve weekday home appearances per year. In 1983, each fan at a game contributed $6–$8 to Dodger gate receipts. Based on these facts plus the information from passage A in the article, what was (at least part of) Valenzuela's expected marginal revenue product for 1983?

2. Do you agree with the arbitrator's decision? Why or why not?

3. In 1982, Valenzuela was paid $350,000. Do you think the Dodgers raised their ticket prices in 1983 because of the increase in Valenzuela's salary? Explain briefly. *Hint:* Is the "Fernando Valenzuela product" the Dodgers are selling to their fans different in quantity or quality because of the change in salary?

Selection Thirty-eight

In reporting on the current "nursing shortage," this article provides an opportunity to practice shifting labor market supply and demand curves in response to recent changes in the nursing market.

Nursing Shortage: Hospitals Feel Effects of Feminism, Low Salaries

THE ASSOCIATED PRESS

BOSTON—A national nursing shortage, the result of the women's movement and lack of high wages, threatens to undermine the medical industry, and the problem in Massachusetts is acute, experts say.

The number of unfilled registered nursing positions in the United States increased from 6.3 percent in 1985 to 13.6 percent in 1987, according to the American Hospital Association, which said that only 17 percent of the 2,300 hospitals it surveyed reported no vacancies.

The Massachusetts Hospital Association found in February that 9 percent of budgeted nursing positions, or 1,600 jobs, were not filled.

"The shortage exists in all parts of the state, and we anticipate it will get more severe this fall or winter," Richard Pozniak, a spokesman for the association, told The Boston Globe.

Boston City Hospital and others have temporarily closed understaffed wards. Faulkner Hospital in Boston and Sturdy Memorial Hospital in Attleboro occasionally divert ambulances to other hospitals.

[A] Faulkner and Mount Auburn Hospital in Cambridge have hired nurses from England, Ireland and other countries.

"Administrators are having to face up to how they can run a hospital without nurses," said Anne Hargreaves, director of the Massachusetts Nursing Association.

[B] The women's movement is cited as one reason for the shortage. Female high school graduates now have more career options than the jobs in nursing and teaching that drew many women in the past.

Today, more women are turning to law, business, medicine and architecture, and men are not moving into nursing at a rate to fill that gap.

Cape Cod Times, July 14, 1987. Copyright 1987, by the Associated Press. Reprinted by permission.

[C] "The focus on helping people swung to a more conservative, self-interested ilk of business," said Patricia Meservey, assistant dean of nursing at Boston University.

[D] Nursing became tougher because under new hospital reimbursement rules, patients must be sicker to be admitted. And the nursing shortage adds to the burden of those still in the profession.

"There's been a speed-up for nurses beyond what they can effectively cope with," said Ms. Hargreaves. "They can't live with the idea they're dealing with life and death issues. . . . They are caught in a kind of burnout."

In most hospitals in the state, overworked nurses focus on the sickest patients and the most pressing problems, leaving less serious demands.

But the big thing is money, say those in the field. Salaries start at $18,000 in rural areas and $23,000 in cities. Top pay is about $35,000, and nurses say that is not enough for the on-the-job stress.

"We may need to pay 20 to 40 percent more," said Linda Shyavitz, president of Sturdy Memorial Hospital. "We have got to provide incentives to get people to think about this field again."

Nursing shortages happen every decade or so, but experts say the current shortage is worse and less likely to improve.

[E] There are fewer young people to become nurses, and more old people needing care. And, nursing schools are going out of business.

Brigham and Women's and some other Boston hospitals have stopped training nurses, and Boston University plans to close its 46-year-old nursing school at the end of the coming academic year.

[F] Hospitals are trying to meet the challenge with more flexible working conditions. Brigham and Women's pays nurses for 40 hours if they work consecutive

83

evening shifts during weekends and for 36 hours for working two weekend day shifts.

Sen. Edward M. Kennedy, D-Mass., has sponsored a bill to establish model recruitment, training and benefit programs for nurses nationwide.

But, he said, without more far-reaching changes, there could be 40 percent fewer nurses than needed by 1990. ∎

QUESTIONS

1. Passages A through F in this article describe various changes in the market for nurses. Considering each passage separately, use a supply and demand diagram for nurses to indicate the effects of *each* passage.
2. Now consider the title of this article:
   a. Based on the title alone, use a supply and demand diagram to indicate what is occurring in the nursing market.
   b. If the wages paid to nurses responded freely and quickly to the forces of supply and demand, would there be a "shortage" and "low salaries"? Explain.

Using actual examples, this article describes some effects of the 1977 rise in the minimum wage. The questions encourage the use of economic analysis to interpret the reported effects of this increase in the price of a variable factor.

Fast-Food Chains Act to Offset the Effects of Minimum-Pay Rise

By PAUL INGRASSIA

HANOVER PARK, Ill.—Cheryl Anders, an 18-year-old part-time hostess at a Kentucky Fried Chicken restaurant here, won't be losing her job after all.

Earlier this year, executives in the $16 billion-a-year fast-food industry tried to forestall the increase in the federal minimum wage to $2.65 an hour from $2.30 by warning that many people like Miss Anders would have to be laid off. The increase was enacted anyway, and yet few layoffs are likely.

Unions that lobbied for the increase, on the other hand, predicted that people like Miss Anders would get a well-deserved 15% pay increase. And that generally won't be happening, either.

[A] Miss Anders's employer, the KFC subsidiary of Heublein Inc., for example, is tightening work schedules at the stores it owns to help offset the effects of the higher wages. In the case of Miss Anders, she will now be working 18 hours a week instead of 23, and earning about $48 a week after Jan. 1, down from the $53 a week she has been averaging.

"I don't mind getting fewer hours because I have more time for other things," she says. "But some people in the store don't like it."

Coping With Costs

[B] KFC's tighter scheduling is but one example of the steps that fast-food chains are taking to deal with the higher labor costs. Also being considered or implemented are such things as more automation—and, not surprisingly, higher prices.

The fast-food companies aren't the only employers with a lot of workers paid the minimum wage, by any means. The Labor Department estimates that 4.5 million workers will be eligible for the automatic increase to $2.65 an hour on Jan. 1, or about 4.5% of the U.S. labor force. Besides fast-food and other restaurants, the industries feeling the greatest impact will be department and grocery stores, hotels, service stations, cleaners and custodial services. Low-wage manufacturers such as textile and apparel companies will also be hit, the Labor Department says.

The new law calls for further increases in the minimum wage, to $2.90 an hour in 1979, $3.10 in 1980 and $3.35 in 1981. Some states, moreover, have minimums above the federal level.

The fast-food industry, which has seen a tripling of sales since 1970, was clearly alarmed by the potential effects of the new pay increase, as most of its employees earn little more than the minimum wage. Last summer, when the legislation was taking shape, executives of the hamburger and chicken chains were forecasting that hundreds of thousands of teen-agers would be thrown out of work.

Shorter Hours Considered

But such giants as KFC, McDonald's and Hardee's now say they don't plan any layoffs. Instead, for the fast-food industry and its customers, the net result of the minimum-wage increase will generally be that the late-night hamburger probably will become a little harder to find and a few cents costlier to buy.

Not that the pay raise won't cost the U.S. economy any jobs. Even the Carter administration, which strongly backed the increase, estimated it could cost some 90,000 jobs through 1981. But the fast-food chains are planning to avoid layoffs with selective price increases, massive marketing efforts to increase sales volume and technological gains in the kitchen to boost productivity—all on the theory that customers will take more kindly to higher prices than to lousy service.

Mostly because of the higher minimum wage, the fast-food industry's total wage costs are expected to rise about 12% next year, industry analysts say. Wages represent about one-fourth of the restaurant's expenses, so a 12% wage increase means a 3% rise in total costs. And that's about how much prices will go up, analysts predict. Jerrico Inc. recently raised prices in its Long John Silver's restaurants by about 2.5%, indicating the prediction is on target.

Though price rises may average 3% overall, they won't be that amount on all items. McDonald's, for instance, is considering "where we can raise prices without dropping customer acceptance" according to Edward H. Schmitt, president.

Holding the Line

And KFC, beset by flat sales in the last three year's, says it won't raise prices at all. The company won't give figures, but it says reducing off-peak work crews has saved more money than the minimum-wage boost will cost—making a price increase unnecessary.

[C] Instead of just sending some workers home earlier, as KFC is doing, some companies may actually close shop earlier. "With the minimum wage going up, hours that once were marginally profitable might become unprofitable," says John Toby, a vice president of Jerrico, which is considering closing earlier.

Taking another tack, McDonald's has launched a companywide campaign to reduce crew turnover, which now averages three times a year at each restaurant. "Hiring and training costs us money," McDonald's Mr. Schmitt says. "If we can cut down on our turnover, we can reduce a major operating cost."

McDonald's and other companies hope the higher minimum wage will bring in more homemakers, who generally don't come and go as quickly as teen-agers and college students. But "housewives feel out of place working with kids," says Donald Trott, a restaurant analyst with Blyth, Eastman Dillon & Co. "Past minimum-wage increases didn't get them to leave their homes to cook hamburgers or chicken."

Another cost-cutting gambit is a 1974 minimum-wage law provision that allows a restaurant owner to hire up to six students to work up to 20 hours a week at 85% of the minimum wage, provided their work hours don't amount to more than 10% of a company's total.

Because of the six-student limitation, the provision is useless to big employers like the fast-food companies, but it can be attractive to their franchisees. "I hadn't taken advantage of this before, but I plan to now," says Stacy Smith, who owns six Dairy Queen restaurants in Decatur, Ill.

Fast-food chains also will try to offset higher costs by boosting sales. Hardee's recently started a series of discount and two-for-one sales, which it hadn't tried before. Many of the promotions will involve its recently introduced roast-beef sandwich. KFC is switching advertising agencies to try to perk up sales.

Some fast-food chains are turning to machinery to boost productivity. Indianapolis-based Steak n Shake Inc., for example, has installed new automatic cash registers that it expects to save the chain about $840,000 a year by eliminating mistakes—or almost as much as the extra $1 million Steak n Shake expects to pay in higher wages.

Hardee's is getting new cash registers that will be tied into a computer, to track the stores busiest hours and permit more-efficient scheduling.

Bishop Buffets Inc., a chain of 20 cafeterias in the Midwest, is testing overnight slow-cookers to reduce early-morning work to prepare roast beef. The idea is to have some early-shift workers start at 7 a.m. instead of at 6 a.m., cutting their work weeks by five hours. Bishop employees now working 45 hours a week at the minimum wage would get only an extra $2.50 a week— $106 compared with $103.50—after the minimum wage goes up and their hours go down.

The quest for labor-saving machines will continue. "Higher labor costs intensify the search for productivity, and we'll be putting more money into research," says McDonald's Mr. Schmitt. "But I can't tell you that tomorrow we'll be installing machines that cook hamburgers without us having to turn them. It just doesn't work that way." ∎

QUESTIONS

1. Refer to passage A: Without calculating any percentage changes, determine whether the demand by KFC for labor-hours is elastic or inelastic over the wage range in this article. Explain your reasoning.
2. Assuming the fast-food industry was initially in long-run competitive equilibrium, will fast-food prices increase in the *short run* according to economic theory? Explain your reasoning and be sure to indicate which, if any, of the various cost curves of the representative firm will be affected by the increase in labor costs. Also indicate whether the *market* supply and/or demand curves will be affected by the increase in labor costs in the short run.
3. Refer to passage B:
   a. What economic equation expresses the long-run cost-minimizing relationship be-

tween labor and capital prices and productivities? (This is sometimes referred to as the "least-cost condition.")

   b. Is the resource substitution reported in passage B what you would expect on the basis of the least-cost condition? Why or why not?

   c. What other examples of this appear in the remainder of the article?

4. Now consider what will happen in this industry in the long run as a result of the minimum-pay rise. Does economic theory predict that the long-run equilibrium price will be higher than before the increase in the minimum wage? Explain your answer carefully.

5. Refer to the paragraph that precedes passage C (it begins, "And KFC, beset by flat sales. . . ."): If this is actually true, was KFC cost minimizing before the minimum-wage boost? Explain briefly.

6. Refer to passage C: What must be true for a firm's profits to rise by closing earlier as a result of the wage rate increase?

This comparatively old article demonstrates that "good intentions" by Congress in trying to help a particular group of workers can be counterproductive if they ignore the full implications derived from economic analysis. The article describes how various farmers in Michigan responded to tougher federal and state housing standards for migrant workers. The questions concern the response of migrant worker employers and the effects that these tougher and higher standards had on some related product markets.

Housing Dispute Spurs Michigan Farmers to Switch to Machines from Migrant Help

By NORMAN PEARLSTINE

LANSING, Mich.—Michigan growers of fruit and vegetables expect a good harvest this summer. But for the thousands of migrant workers who are expected to stream into the state to help harvest the crops, the pickings are likely to be slim.

Growers are stepping up their use of machines to harvest crops, so there will be fewer jobs available, according to farm-labor authorities here. Housing for the migrants will also be scarcer this summer, mainly because of unwillingness or inability of growers to comply with tougher Federal and state housing standards.

With abundant help from migrant workers (only California uses more of them), Michigan has become the nation's largest producer of red tart cherries, dry beans, pickly cucumbers, blueberries and hothouse rhubarb. Migrants also help gather the state's big crops of apples, grapes, sugar beets, soybeans and potatoes.

But higher labor costs have prompted many growers here and elsewhere throughout the country to switch to mechanized harvesting in recent years, lessening demand for migrant workers. That trend has intensified in the last two years, as government agencies have implemented stricter housing regulations for growers participating in their migrant-worker placement programs.

Many growers say that unfavorable publicity about housing conditions for migrants on some farms prompted them to close down migrant-labor camps and to switch to mechanization. "It might be cheaper for me to continue using migrant help for a few more years," says one western Michigan fruit grower, "but mechanization is the trend of the future. And no matter what kind of housing I provide, I'm going to be criticized for mistreating migrants so I might as well switch now," he adds.

No Variances

Under Federal regulations, growers can't use an interstate farm-labor service unless they meet housing standards set by the Labor Department. These regulations allow for variances from the standards if they don't create a health or safety hazard. Michigan growers assert that last winter the Labor Department's regional officer in Chicago decided against allowing any variances.

Several growers in western Michigan reacted by circulating petitions throughout the state demanding that variances be granted and that the state and Federal government provide aid to growers who had to make large capital expenditures to upgrade their migrant camps. Other growers exerted political pressure on the legislators in Michigan and Washington to get the standards relaxed. About 10,000 persons signed the petitions and in mid-April officials of the Labor Department in Washington agreed that variances should be allowed.

Many other growers, however, simply decided that they wouldn't participate in the interstate service this year and wouldn't submit their housing to the scrutiny of officials. Joseph C. Kaspar, Chicago regional director for the Farm-Labor and Rural-Manpower Service, says that variances and interstate orders have been granted to almost any grower who has asked for them. But there have been relatively few applications, he adds.

Sharp Reductions

The lack of work contracts and the relative scarcity of jobs has been particularly severe in the Saginaw-Bay City area of the state, where many sugar-beet growers mechanized this year and closed their migrant camps. Roy Fuentes, a member of the Office of Economic Opportunity here, says that the Saginaw–Bay City area "is very short of migrant housing," and he adds that "it will be a pretty rough summer" for migrants throughout the state.

Donald E. Holtzman, a South Haven blueberry farmer, says that he used as many as 150 migrants three years ago to help harvest his crop, but that he plans to use fewer than a dozen this summer.

State and Federal officials estimate that mechanization could eliminate from 6,000 to 10,000 jobs in Michigan this summer that were previously done by migrants. Norman Papsdorf, chief of the Michigan Department of Health's agricultural labor-camps unit, which licenses all the state's migrant labor camps, says license applications are down 11% so far this summer to 1,575 from 1,775 a year ago.

Nonetheless, approximately 50,000 migrant workers, mostly Mexican-Americans from southwest Texas, are expected to come into Michigan looking for work this summer. That's about the same number that came through last year. Their slimmer chances of finding available work and shelter have been aggravated by an apparent breakdown here in the Federal-state program for interstate recruitment of migrants.

In recent years more than half of the migrants

coming into the state have been recruited and placed in jobs and living camps by the Michigan Employment Security Commission, a Federally supported state agency that works closely with the Labor Department. Last year the commission's farm-labor rural-manpower service arranged jobs and housing for 27,163 workers. But this year commission officials say that "we're only going to place about 7,000 or 8,000 workers." The rest of the migrants coming into the state will have to find their own work and shelter.

The growers' decision against using the interstate service this summer stems primarily from the heated battle they had with state and Federal authorities earlier this year over interpretation of the Federal housing standards.

Mr. Fuentes says that the state may try to go into the housing business itself, leasing accommodations to migrants. In addition, the Michigan Economic Opportunity Office has announced that it will set up at least 17 area councils throughout the state to establish a number of centers providing food, medical and dental care for migrants.

Meanwhile, agriculture experts here say they see good crop prospects. Weather has been good and pollination of fruit trees successful throughout most of the state. Although it is too early to forecast crop prices, most authorities say that this year's crop revenue should match last year's respectable showing, when the state's growers received about $70 million for their fruit and about $57 million for their vegetables.

The Michigan Crop Reporting Service, a statistical bureau supported by the state and Federal agriculture departments, has forecast that this year's tart-cherry crop will be about 1,000 tons less than the 106,000 tons harvested last year, while the sweet cherry crop is predicted to increase 1,000 tons to 23,000 tons. Bigger peach and pear crops also are predicted.

The reporting services hasn't yet made its forecast for commercial apples, the state's most valuable fruit crop. But some industry sources are looking for this year's apple harvest to be at least as good as last year when about 680 million pounds of apples worth about $27 million were picked. Michigan ranks third among apple-producing states. ∎

QUESTIONS

1. Explain carefully, using economic theory, the Michigan farmers' response to stricter housing standards. In your explanation be sure to use the economic equation expressing the long-run cost-minimizing relationship between labor and capital prices and productivities (sometimes referred to as the "least-cost condition").

2. What effect do you think the stricter housing

standards will have on the prices of goods produced by the farmers affected by this legislation? Explain your answer using economic theory.

3. Whom do you see as being helped by these stricter housing standards? Whom do you see as being hurt? Include in your answer each of the following groups: (a) migrant workers, (b) farmers, (c) consumers, and (d) producers of mechanized farm equipment.

College athletes, often perceived as unduly pampered, may in fact be victims of monopsonistic exploitation. This article reports on the revenues generated by a number of prominent college athletes without pointing out the possible monopsony situation. The questions accompanying the article consider the contrast between the income and the marginal revenue products of top college athletes.

When a College Signs a Franchise, Benefits Can Spill Out Everywhere

By ROBERT JOHNSON and MARK RUSSELL

CINCINNATI—This year's University of Cincinnati basketball team was expected to be yet another doormat on the court and a drain on the school budget.

Instead, the team enters its conference championships today with an outside chance of qualifying for the NCAA playoffs—a feat that would net $141,000. The brilliant play of freshman guard Roger McClendon has sparked the turnaround, and this city and school are still reeling.

People are scrounging for tickets while donations pour in from alumni who haven't been heard from in years. The university's long admissions decline has reversed itself. Local restaurants are swamped by post-game crowds. Stores are running low on Bearcat sweatshirts. And a glut of office space near the team's arena is suddenly marketable. "Basketball is part of the downtown revitalization," says Steve Wilson, president of a local company.

The impact of Mr. McClendon illustrates the marketing importance of the unique player—in sporting parlance, the franchise—to college athletic programs. Much more than glory is at stake: Large TV contracts and lucrative tournament berths are dangled before the nation's best teams. And profits from successful sports operations benefit schools' academic programs. "I'm becoming a commodity," says Mr. McClendon. "People are depending on me."

Million-Dollar Contracts

To be sure, a strong element of personal self-interest is present. Doug Flutie brought $3 million in television revenues and a 33% increase in admissions

applications to Boston College in his last two years starring at quarterback. He, in turn, landed a $7 million contract with United States Football League's New Jersey Generals.

The college basketball franchise player, however, usually has a more immediate economic impact than his football counterpart, given his higher visibility among fewer players and his sport's relatively small budget. Charisma counts.

Consider the University of Oklahoma. In 1981–82, the basketball team had a 22–11 record and went to the National Invitational Tournament. But absent a big star, the Sooners never made national TV, and the basketball program lost about $80,000 on a $500,000 budget.

But then came Wayman Tisdale. In 1982–83 the flashy center made Oklahoma a marketable commodity. The team has been on national TV 14 times in the Tisdale era, and on the strength of big conference broadcast fees and doubled season-ticket sales, basketball earned $200,000 in his first year and $350,000 in his second.

Moreover, Oklahoma's Tip-In Club, a basketball booster group, saw its membership more than triple to 1,400 this season from 430 before Mr. Tisdale arrived. Member contributions nearly quadrupled to $160,000 this season from $45,000 in 1980–81.

The arrival in 1979 of Steve Stipanovich, a heralded center, at the University of Missouri, catapulted that school into national basketball prominence. In his first season, average home-game attendance surged 43% to 9,460 from 6,624. Missouri, which wasn't offered a national or regional television appearance in the three years before Mr. Stipanovich's arrival, made 57 such appearances in his four seasons.

Losing a Job

Missouri's basketball program earned $250,000 in Mr. Stipanovich's last season after breaking even the previous four years. "Basketball wasn't carrying its head above water before (Stipanovich)," says Dave Hart, the university's athletic director.

One basketball player can make or break a coach. For instance, Abe Lemons, now coach at Oklahoma City University, was fired by the University of Texas after the 1982–83 season. The team jumped to a 14–0 start that year, led by sophomore star Mike Wacker. But Mr. Wacker injured his knee, and the team lost 11 of its last 13 games.

"Before the athletic director fired me, he asked, 'Coach, can one man make that much difference?'" recalls Mr. Lemons. "The answer is yes. One special player can be the difference between winning and losing."

The University of Cincinnati desperately needed a franchise player. Poor management had weakened a program that had won national championships in 1961 and 1962. Fund-raising efforts lagged, and the basketball team continued to play in a cramped 7,800-seat fieldhouse while other schools built huge arenas that attracted more fans and top players.

Cincinnati has also missed the current college basketball boom. Today, network and cable TV compete to televise top teams, some of whom make several appearances annually at up to $90,000 a game. But Cincinnati, wracked by recruiting violations, a coaching turnover and losing seasons, hasn't made a network television appearance since 1982. Operating losses have totaled about $50,000 annually since 1980.

Searching for a new coach after the 1982–83 season, Cincinnati took a chance on Tony Yates, who starred on the school's championship teams in the 1960s. Fresh from the University of Illinois, Mr. Yates had his eye on a turnaround catalyst: a 6-foot 4-inch local schoolboy named Roger McClendon.

Last year, while waiting for Mr. McClendon to complete high school in Illinois, Mr. Yates finished with a record of three wins and 25 losses. But this season Mr. McClendon is in large measure the Wunderkind Cincin-

nati hoped for. He has sparked upset wins over highly ranked University of Alabama-Birmingham and arch-rival University of Louisville in leading the team to a 15–12 record.

Problems in School

Being a franchise, however, exacts a toll. Mr. McClendon, a near-straight-A student in high school, is struggling with his courses at Cincinnati. He aspires to be a Rhodes scholar, but each week's regimen of 18 hours practice and two games, with travel ranging from Florida to California, eats into study time and saps his concentration. "I let a lot of people down," he said after a recent loss to Memphis State. "But I'll bounce back. I know I will."

The university is pulling for him. The Charles Mc-Mikan Society, an elite friends-of-the-university club, has seen membership swell 17% this year—with entry costing a minimum donation of $1,000. Says the group's chairman, William J. Parchman, "Winning basketball games just helps along the feeling of giving."

School officials also give basketball much of the credit for a resurgence in freshman admissions—up 10% from a year ago, after a steady decline since 1980. And long-lost graduates are calling the alumni association after games to ask for scores, says executive director Chris Demakes. They get the scores, the association gets callers' addresses, and fund-raising pleas will soon go out to the rediscovered alumni.

The graduates will be asked to contribute to a planned $16 million fieldhouse. The hook: photos of Mr. McClendon, tales of his prowess and visions of nationally televised games in the completed facility. "Roger's a name-potential player," says George Wolterman, the university's associate athletic director. "We'll market around him."

The school is already recruiting around him. The allure of Mr. McClendon has already helped Mr. Yates sign a promising 6-foot 10-inch center. And despite the chances of success in the championships today, thoughts are mostly on next year. Talk of the team's first TV appearance since 1982 pleases Mr. Wolterman. "Once TV decides you're a top-20 team," he says, "your fans do too, and the money starts rolling in." ■

QUESTIONS

1. During their college years, what do athletes such as Roger McClendon and Doug Flutie receive as compensation for their efforts?
2. Do you think Doug Flutie was paid his marginal revenue product as a college athlete? Support your answer.
3. Some economists claim that the NCAA is an example of a "monopsony." Indicate whether you agree, making use of evidence from the article to support your answer.

Throughout their lives, when buying "large-ticket" items, consumers confront financing choices that can be better made with the help of present-value analysis. This selection is an advertisement for GMAC's auto-financing options. The ad sets up an example, and it provides enough information for buyers to make the "right" choice.

1.9% APR

Chevrolet's advertisement appears on page 94.

QUESTIONS

Consider a consumer who buys the Chevy Cavalier discussed in the last paragraph of the ad. Suppose the buyer considers two options:

   a. Pay cash and get the cash rebate indicated in the first table of the ad, or
   b. Pay 10 percent down and use Chevy's two-year financing plan. (For simplicity, assume that each year's twelve monthly payments are all made at year-end.)

For each of the following two questions, be sure to indicate how you arrived at your decision.

1. If the buyer is earning 5 percent on her savings, which option should she choose?
2. If the buyer is earning 10 percent on her savings, which option should she choose?

Courtesy of General Motors Corporation.

1.9% APR
At this rate, it's so easy to drive a new Chevy home.

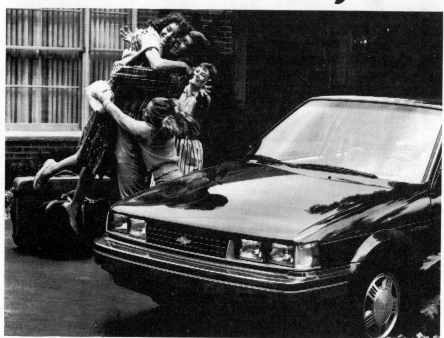

The Big One's back!

1.9% APR, GMAC's best financing plan ever, just could be the best reason to drive a new Chevrolet home right now.

OR, you can choose to get a sizable amount —up to $700—of cash back on the select Chevy of your choice. You must take actual retail delivery out of dealer stock by September 30, 1987. Dealer financial participation may affect consumer cost.

The Big One's back. And Chevy's got it. It's yours on an enormous selection of Chevrolets. And it just could be one of the best opportunities you'll ever find on four wheels. So see your participating Chevy dealer for qualification details now. And then—

just listen to your heartbeat.

For example, if you finance a Cavalier with a Manufacturer's Suggested Retail Price of $8763.00* and a 10% down payment, the following rates would apply:

THE BIG CHEVY CHOICE.	THE BIG CASH-BACK BONUS.
Beretta ('88)	$350
Corsica ('88)	$350
Sprint	$500
Spectrum	$700
Spectrum Express	$300
Nova	$500
Cavalier	$600
Camaro	$350
Celebrity	$700
Caprice	$350

THE BIGGEST FINANCING PLAN GMAC HAS EVER OFFERED.				
APR	LENGTH OF CONTRACT	AMOUNT FINANCED	MONTHLY PAYMENT	TOTAL FINANCE SAVINGS†
1.9%	24 MOS.	$7886.70	$335.15	$ 842.64
3.9%	36 MOS.	$7886.70	$232.49	$1023.84
4.8%	48 MOS.	$7886.70	$180.91	$1235.04
8.9%	60 MOS.	$7886.70	$163.33	$ 661.80

*Cavalier with A.C., tinted glass, sport mirrors, power steering and body-side molding options. Does not include license, taxes or customer-selected service and insurance.

†Based on the average finance rate of 11.73% for vehicles financed by GMAC and not eligible for a special rate for the month of July 1987.

GM 6/60 QUALITY COMMITMENT PLAN

Let's get it together... buckle up.

See your Chevrolet dealer for terms and conditions of the limited warranty. 6/60 not available on Sprint or Spectrum.

THE *Heartbeat* OF AMERICA ⬡ TODAY'S CHEVROLET
See your local Chevy dealer.

Most large state lottery prizes are paid out over several years, but lottery officials never publicize how much the prizes are worth in present-value terms. This article applies present-value analysis to lottery prizes and even includes a table showing the present value of each payment of a $1 million prize spread out over twenty years.

State's Lottery 'Millionaires' Will Be Somewhat Less Than

By LEE DEMBART

When the California lottery gets into full swing this fall, it will offer jackpots of $1 million, $2 million and $3 million. The lucky winners, therefore, will be "millionaires," according to common parlance.

Not so fast. There's a rub. "All million-dollar prizes will be awarded as annuities over a 20-year period," said an article in The Times. In other words, if you win, say, a million dollars, the Lottery Commission won't hand you a check for a million. It will pay you $50,000 now and promise to pay another $50,000 a year for 19 more years, for a total of $1 million.

Now, $50,000 a year for 20 years is not worth a million dollars by a long shot. In fact, according to Bill Seaton, spokesman for the Lottery Commission, if you win "a million dollars" in the lottery, what they actually will give you is not a million dollars but an annuity worth $400,000 today.

A $400,000 annuity winds up being worth $1 million over 20 years because of the miracle of compound interest. Think about it. Money that is put aside today earns interest and is worth more in the future. The longer the future is, the more it grows.

So if the state promises to pay you $50,000 19 years from now—the time of the last payment—how much does it have to put aside today in order to have the $50,000 then? It depends, obviously, on the interest rate. The higher the interest rate, the less that has to be set aside initially. If it earns 8%, $11,585.60 will yield $50,000 in 19 years. At a 10% rate, $8,175.40 will grow to $50,000 in 19 years. And at 12%, it would take just $5,805.34 today to produce $50,000 in 2004.

This is a well-known bit of straightforward mathematics, which is called the present-value or present-worth calculation. It involves running the formula for compound interest backward, and it answers the question, "What is the present value of a future sum of money?" Everybody understands that if a person invested $1,000 today at 10% interest it would earn $100 in a year and then be worth $1,100. The question can be asked the other way: If you wind up with $1,100 in a

Year	Payment	Present value
0	$50,000	$50,000.00
1	50,000	44,326.24
2	50,000	39,296.31
3	50,000	34,837.16
4	50,000	30,884.00
5	50,000	27,379.44
6	50,000	24,272.55
7	50,000	21,518.22
8	50,000	19,076.43
9	50,000	16,911.73
10	50,000	14,992.67
11	50,000	13,291.38
12	50,000	11,783.13
13	50,000	10,446.04
14	50,000	9,260.67
15	50,000	8,209.82
16	50,000	7,278.21
17	50,000	6,452.31
18	50,000	5,720.13
19	50,000	5,071.04

year at 10% interest, how much did you start with? The answer is $1,000, and that is called the present value of $1,100 in a year at 10% interest.

Occasionally, when athletes sign multi-year, multi-million-dollar contracts, someone points out that an owner who promises to pay $2 million 30 years from now can do it with much less than $2 million today.

How does the lottery figure the present value of $1 million doled out in 20-year installments of $50,000 a year? The same calculation that is done for year 19—the last year—can also be done for years 18, 17, 16 and so on to determine the amount of money that must be set aside today to pay the $50,000 in each of the subsequent years. Then those present values can be added to yield the total present value of the state's "million-dollar lottery." The following is a table showing the present values of 20 once-a-year payments of $50,000 each, assuming earnings of 12.8%:

The total present value of $1 million handed out in $50,000 chunks over 20 years is $401,007.48.

So it is at least misleading to call $50,000 a year for 20 years "a million dollars." (This analysis ignores income tax, inflation, life expectancy and all other factors related to the question of which is the better deal, $400,000 today or $50,000 a year for 20 years.)

[A] The Lottery Commission says further that, based on the same calculation, a winner of a $2-million jackpot will receive an $800,000 annuity. In addition, the commission says, the odds against winning a $2-million pot are 25 million to 1.

So a person who buys a $1 ticket will have a 25 million-to-1 shot at winning a "$2-million" prize. That sounds like bad odds to begin with. The odds are made worse by the fact that the $2-million prize is really only $800,000. ■

QUESTIONS

1. Use the article's table of present values to help you answer the following questions:
   a. Why does the present value of each $50,000 payment fall continuously in successive years?
   b. How much would a $5 million lottery prize actually cost the state to finance?
   c. What would happen to the cost to the state of the "$1 million" lottery prize if
      (1) The interest rate was lower than 12.8 percent?
      (2) The payout period was shorter than twenty years?
2. How would you determine the present value of a $50,000 payment made at the end of two years if the interest rate is 12.8 percent the first year and 10 percent the second? (Set up the appropriate computation without solving for the actual number.)
3. Based on the information in passage A:
   a. What is the expected return on a $1 "investment" in a lottery ticket?
   b. Is buying two lottery tickets a better "investment" than buying one? Explain briefly.
4. Consider a $5 million" lottery prize, paid out in equal payments over the next twenty years. Is it false advertising to label the prize "$5 million"? Explain briefly.

This article illustrates seriously flawed reasoning attributable to a failure to consider the concept of present value when acquiring a solar hot-water heater for the White House.

Carter Sees Solar Heater as Example and Symbol

By RACHELLE PATTERSON

WASHINGTON—President Jimmy Carter is about to set a shining example.

He is having a solar hot-water heater installed on the roof of the west wing of the White House in an effort to save energy.

Since Washington has an average of 159 cloudy days and 11 rainy days a year, the unit's effectiveness is sure to be watched with interest by other of the nation's less sunny climes, like New England.

At his news conference last week, Carter said he hoped "we're considered an example for the rest of the nation" in conservation of energy. He cited his family's living with lower thermostat settings and a shift at the White House to smaller cars. Although he went to Georgia for a vacation, Carter said White House travel is limited to official business.

The solar unit, which will be seen by visiting tourists, is regarded as a symbol. It is, he said, one of a few "personal things to demonstrate our belief in the principles" outlined in his energy speech earlier this month.

The goal of the heater is to produce 90.4 million BTUs annually, according to William Corcoran of the Energy Department's solar unit. To produce that much heat electrically would cost $2600 a year. The cost of the unit, which is supposed to last 25 years, is $28,000. Thus, the savings is supposed to be $1480 a year.

The unit 611 square feet in size and containing 32 collectors, will heat water tanks in the west wing behind the Oval office. It is supposed to provide 75 percent of the hot-water requirements for the Cabinet room, bathroom and the White House mess, which are all in the west wing.

Should Washington weather be unusually bad and the collectors unable to bank sufficient energy from the sunny days, the back-up, electrical system will help out.

The heater's inaugural is planned for the end of April. ∎

QUESTIONS

1. How does the Energy Department arrive at its conclusion that buying the solar heating unit for $28,000 will result in a savings of $1,480 per year?
2. Accepting the costs of electricity and of the solar heater as given in the article, what has the Energy Department overlooked in calculating the savings from installing the solar heater? *Hint:* How might the concept of present value apply here?
3. Suppose the White House pays its electric bill of $2,600 at the end of each year. Suppose further that the White House has a very large bank account that earns 10 percent interest per year. Does it really make economic sense for the White House to use $28,000 of its savings to buy the solar heating unit? Why or why not?
4. If the interest rate were lower than 10 percent, how might this affect your answer in question 3? What if the interest rate were higher than 10 percent? Explain.

The Boston Globe, April 1979. Reprinted courtesy of The Boston Globe.

The information in this article permits the use of economic analysis to try to sort out the real source of recent college tuition increases. In addition, consideration is given to the question of how one might rationally make the investment decision about obtaining a B.A. degree, and the application of the concept of present value in such a decision.

Benefit of B.A. Is Greater Than Ever

By GARY PUTKA

There may be something rising faster than the price of going to college, after all.

The price of not going.

In a ritual well known to strapped parents, the College Board recently released its annual survey showing tuitions rising faster than inflation. As is customary, the big admissions group gave no explanation for the 7% increase for 1988–89, the eighth year in a row that the rise in college tuition has outpaced inflation.

Pressed by Congress and others for the reasons, colleges have in the past blamed the need for more scholarships and higher faculty salaries. But a growing body of research suggests a more markets-like answer: College costs more because the product is worth more.

Measured in terms of income, returns on a bachelor's degree "have been exploding in the '80s," says Finis Welch, an economics professor at the University of California at Los Angeles who specializes in the labor market. Mr. Welch and other analysts, using census data, see a dramatic rise in the amount of income gained by going to college over a time period roughly coinciding with the big tuition increases.

Salary Gap

Male college graduates in the work force made 39.2% more than high school graduates in 1986, the latest year of Census Bureau reports, compared with 23.8% in 1979. For women, the difference rose to 40.5% from 27.9%.

More recent data, derived by University of Michigan economist Jonathan Bound from computer tapes of the Census Bureau's monthly surveys, indicate that the differences were more pronounced in 1987. Mr. Bound's figures show that the gap last year was 70%

for women in their first 10 working years and 46% for males of that experience. Economists caution that when data for all workers is reported by the Census Bureau, the unusually large gap for women will probably shrink, though it still will be above the 1986 figure.

Moreover, Mr. Bound says the figures don't reflect another benefit of college, namely that the college educated are less likely to be unemployed than high school graduates. And Mr. Welch's research shows that the gap between more-seasoned workers is widening even faster, peaking at about 20 years' experience and remaining steady afterward.

No one is sure what's behind the growing income gap, but some economists point to a drop in high-paying factory jobs among high school graduates. Another reason may be the growing importance of high-tech employment demanding more education. Also, while the number of new college graduates has edged up only about 5% in the past 10 years to about 980,000 a year, the work force has expanded much faster. This has given a sheepskin a rarity value unimagined in the 1970s, when the well-educated flooded the labor market and the cabbie with a doctorate drove his way into national folklore.

"It's rather remarkable," says Richard Freeman, an economist whose 1976 book, "The Overeducated American," presented evidence on the decline of a diploma's value. Now director of labor studies at the national Bureau for Economic Research in Boston, Mr. Freeman says he had expected college's value to make a comeback, "but no one anticipated the magnitude" of the gains for college graduates.

[A] Census data show that the median income of the college-educated man in 1986 was $34,391 versus $24,701 for those without college. That means that the college "payback time"—the number of years it takes a worker to recoup four years of tuition and lost earnings—has shrunk despite the soaring tuitions. Using tui-

---

Comparing the median income of college educated men and women and high school educated men and women. (in thousands of dollars)

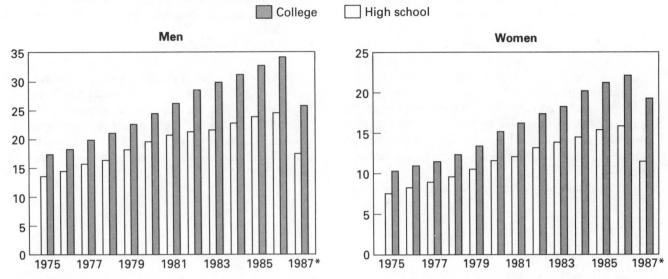

College ▢ High school

*Includes only workers out of school 10 years or less, based on census data analyzed by Jonathan Bound, University of Michigan.

Source: Bureau of the Census

tion figures for public colleges, which educate about 77% of all students, the payback time is down to about 11 years, from about 17 in 1979, before the big tuition mark-ups.

Economists don't suggest that high school seniors are delving through census data and punching calculators before deciding whether or not to attend college. But they do say students and parents know what's going on around them—and act accordingly.

"People see some of the kind of job creation that's going on, and they realize without a college education they're up a tree," says Louis Morrell, treasurer of Radcliffe College, Cambridge, Mass. "People want it and they're willing to pay for it."

Relatively stable annual enrollment of about 12 million students in the 1980s wouldn't seem to support the idea of more clamoring for college. But enrollment has held steady in the face of a 16% decline in the number of high school graduates since 1977. More college freshmen than ever say they're there to make more money, and according to the most recent Gallup survey on the subject, 64% of Americans rate a college education as "very important" in getting ahead, up from 36% in 1978.

"Costs have escalated at the very moment in history when more people believe that (college) is worth it," says Terry Hartle, education aide to Sen. Edward Kennedy of Massachusetts. "I don't think it's unrelated."

High Cost of College
Average annual price of four-year colleges

	Tuition and Fees	
	Public	Private
1977–78	$ 621	$2,476
1978–79	651	2,647
1979–80	680	2,923
1980–81	706	3,279
1981–82	819	3,709
1982–83	979	4,021
1983–84	1,105	4,627
1984–85	1,126	5,016
1985–86	1,242	5,418
1986–87	1,337	5,793
1987–88*	1,359	7,110
1988–89*	1,566	7,693

NOTE: Figures are as reported in year of survey
*Weighted averages; all others unweighted
Source: College Board

Market Forces

The figures tend to support the economic value of college. But they also suggest that prices in higher education are more subject to market forces than universities have generally acknowledged. Richard Rosser, president of the National Association of Independent Colleges and Universities, says many colleges struggle to hold the line on costs without sacrificing quality. And he adds that tuitions cover only a portion of total costs, with the balance coming from governments, private donations and investment earnings. "Colleges agonize over tuition decisions," he says. "What they're doing is simply covering the real cost of running our universities."

With soaring applications, officials of Ivy League and other top private colleges have long contended that they could raise tuitions by more than they have, and still retain enrollments. They say they have resisted doing so because of concern about the ability of some people to pay.

As for the future?

Higher tuitions still, say the economists who study higher education, until quality, or at least the economic value of higher education, is perceived to decline. "Colleges will act like businessmen on a board," says Mr. Morrell of Radcliffe. "They price themselves according to what the value of the good is perceived to be, and they'll continue to do that until the market says it won't accept it." ∎

QUESTIONS

1. How does each of the following affect the "salaries" for college graduates relative to those for high school graduates? Use a supply and demand diagram for each group to support your answers.
   a. A drop in high-paying factory jobs among high school graduates.
   b. The growing importance of high-tech employment which requires more education.
   c. The number of new college graduates has edged up only about 5 percent in the past ten years while the number of people in the work force has expanded much faster.
2. How, if at all, is the situation reported in the article consistent with your analysis above?
3. Show the effect of higher B.A. salaries on a supply and demand diagram for college attendance. In particular, what is the effect on (a) tuition and (b) the number of students attending college?
4. According to the article, colleges have in the past blamed higher tuition on higher costs in the form of higher faculty salaries and more scholarships:
   a. What effect would "higher costs of faculty" by itself have on (1) tuition and (2) the number of students attending college? Illustrate your answer by using an appropriate supply and demand diagram for college attendance.
   b. What effect would higher B.A. salaries have on college faculty salaries? Illustrate your answer with an appropriate supply and demand diagram of college faculty.
   c. There appear to be two alternative explanations for the increase in college tuition: (1) higher faculty salaries versus (2) the increased value of going to college. Based on your answers to questions 3 and 4a as well as the information in this article, which alternative seems to be at work? Explain your answer.
5. Consider passage A:
   a. What is the meaning of the term "payback time"?
   b. Suppose college attendance were viewed solely as an "investment decision," with the only benefit being the additional income it generated for the student in the future. If the "payback" time as defined in passage A were eleven years, would you go to college if you expected to work exactly eleven more years? Why or why not? Hint: Think about the concept of present value.
   c. Again assuming college attendance is an "investment decision," how would you account for the fact that college students tend to be younger people?

This editorial argues for raising the price of local calls from a public phone from a dime to a quarter. The questions apply the traditional economic criteria of (allocative) efficiency and equity (distribution) to this issue.

Why Calls Should Cost a Quarter

A *quarter* for a coin phone?

Local calls from a public phone already cost a quarter in 19 states and 20 cents in 13 others. But New Yorkers are deeply attached to the dime call. Seven times in 14 years, politically minded regulators have denied appeals for an increase.

Some intracity calls were finally designated to cost 30 cents, but most still go for a dime, the same price charged in 1951. So New York Telephone is back, asking for a quarter, and now, more than ever before, the Public Service Commission should relent. Pay-phone service costs the company nearly three times the dime it charges. There is simply no justification for requiring all other phone users to make up the difference.

When New York's pay-phone calls went from a nickel to a dime, a first-class letter cost 3 cents and a subway ride 15 cents. Why, then, the emotional resistance to paying more for a call?

Once upon a time, the protesters could claim that an additional charge might jeopardize public safety: The lack of an extra coin might prevent people from calling the police or fire department. But today, almost all pay phones allow emergency dialing without any coin, and the remaining 6 percent will be converted within two years.

[A] New York Attorney General Robert Abrams has another objection. He says higher coin-phone charges would harm the poor, who lack phones of their own. Yet 97 percent of all New Yorkers, including most poor people, have access to a home phone. And the overwhelming majority of pay-phone calls are made by people of average means or better—travelers and people en route to work.

Keeping pay phones cheap means offsetting the losses with an extra $1.20 monthly charge on all other phones. Most of the beneficiaries of that are middle-income customers, and some of the biggest losers are poor people with home phones. The better, more direct way to assure universal access to a phone is to approve the proposed "lifeline" service, offering home phones and a severely limited number of calls for about $4 a month.

Easy access to coin phones is an invaluable convenience. But there's no reason to keep asking homeowners in Plattsburg and shopkeepers in the Bronx to subsidize the convenience of commuters at Grand Central Terminal. ∎

QUESTIONS

1. Based on the material in this editorial, what is the efficient price for local calls from a public phone? Explain your answer with the aid of a diagram.
2. Why is the current ten-cent price inefficient? Are there too few or too many local calls from public phones with this pricing scheme?
3. Consider a price held below the competitive equilibrium level:
   a. What happens to the quantity supplied in a perfectly competitive market under such circumstances?
   b. What happens to the quantity supplied by the regulated phone company under these same circumstances?
   c. What, do you think, accounts for the difference above?
4. Who would gain and who would lose from the pricing change being advocated here? Explain your reasoning, making any assumptions explicit. How does your answer compare with that of New York Attorney General Robert Abrams in passage A?

This article deals with externalities and the question of whether there would be any "market failure" if the market for billboards and storefront signs were unregulated. After explicitly asking students to consider this issue, the questions focus on what policies are most advantageous from the standpoint of achieving the efficient quantities of such goods as billboards and storefront signs.

Braude's Ban on New Billboards Falls One Vote Short

By RICHARD SIMON

An effort to ban new billboards in Los Angeles was narrowly defeated by the City Council Tuesday amid contentious debate and heavy lobbying from the sign industry.

The measure fell one vote short of the eight required for approval.

Councilman Marvin Braude, who has sought to ban billboards for 16 years, vowed to continue the fight.

"This isn't going to go away," Braude told his colleagues.

"In 1972, I got four votes. Today, I got seven votes," he added in an interview after the vote. "That's tremendous progress. During the next few years, we'll increase it so that we'll have the majority. I'm optimistic."

Gerald Silver, president of Homeowners of Encino, said he and other members of a coalition of chambers of commerce and homeowner groups that pushed for the ban will mount an intensive lobbying campaign to pick up an eighth vote. If that fails, he said, supporters may go directly to the voters with an initiative.

Encino homeowners have been in the forefront of the proposed ban because of 33 billboards and 1,500 smaller signs along a 3½-mile stretch of Ventura Boulevard in their community. The measure would also have strengthened the city's law restricting storefront signs.

During the emotional two-hour debate, Councilman Hal Bernson argued that a ban on new billboards would "destroy an entire industry."

But Councilwoman Joy Picus, citing a number of other cities, such as Beverly Hills, Santa Barbara and Santa Monica that have banned the signs, said, "The beautiful cities are the ones without billboards."

Braude, who sponsored the proposed ban, attributed the defeat to heavy lobbying by the billboard industry, a major contributor to council members' political campaigns. While industry lobbyists conferred with council members on the side of the chamber, 300 employees of billboard companies packed the room.

Free Space

Representatives of billboard companies also presented the council with a 3-foot-high stack of about 2,000 letters from such groups as the Los Angeles County Medical Assn., which received free billboard space to encourage the use of condoms to help prevent the spread of acquired immune deficiency syndrome.

Braude has lost three previous efforts to ban new billboards. (State law prohibits cities from outlawing existing billboards without compensating billboard companies.) But this time, proponents of a ban were encouraged by a number of changes in the political climate, including the burgeoning slow-growth movement and last year's defeat of Council President Pat Russell, a leading foe of tougher sign controls, by environmentalist Ruth Galanter.

Billboard companies argued that the city's 2-year-old sign law, limiting the distance of billboards from each other and residences, works.

Ken Spiker, a former city legislative analyst who is now a lobbyist for four billboard companies, said that since the law went into effect in July, 1986, his clients have taken down 481 billboards and put up only 84 new ones.

No Assurance

But sign-control advocates contend that the existing law permits thousands of new billboards to go up.

If one is torn down, there is no assurance that a new one will not go up on the same site, they say.

The Los Angeles County–Orange County area ranks first in the nation in billboards, with an estimated 22,000, nearly twice the number in the second-ranked New York metropolitan area, an industry source said. Of those, about 9,500 billboards are in the city of Los Angeles, the Planning Department said.

The roll call on Braude's ordinance was:

For: Ernani Bernardi, Joan Milke Flores, Galanter, Mike Woo, Zev Yaroslavsky, Braude and Picus.

Against: Richard Alatorre, John Ferraro, Robert Farrell, Gilbert W. Lindsay, Nate Holden, Gloria Molina, Joel Wachs and Bernson.

QUESTIONS

1. What does economic analysis say about the quantity of billboards that would be efficient?
2. Would you expect that a private, unregulated market would result in an efficient number of billboards in Los Angeles? Why or why not?
3. In light of your answer to the above questions, when would a total ban result in the efficient number of billboards? That is, when would zero billboards be the efficient number? Explain carefully with the aid of a diagram.
4. How would you respond to the argument that one benefit of the billboard industry is the jobs it creates for employees of billboard companies?

This article serves as a good vehicle for evaluating the economic arguments for government aid to finance college students. It reports on the 1981 moves in Congress to reduce federal aid along the lines recommended by then President Ronald Reagan.

The Cuts in Federal Aid

By JERROLD K. FOOTLICK with LUCY HOWARD, RICHARD MANNING, and DAVID FINK

Missouri Valley College, in the quiet town of Marshall, Mo., is a picture-book Midwestern school with 500 students. It is inexpensive as private colleges go: only $4,272 last year for room, board and tuition. But many of its students come from nearby farms and small towns, where there isn't a lot of spare money around. Eighteen-year-old Cyndy Sullivan is typical. This summer she will complete her sophomore year, thanks to work, ingenuity, helpful college officials, a bank and the Federal government. Cyndy earned $994 working for the minimum wage in the admissions office; she won an $850 merit scholarship for good grades; she received a $1,088.50 scholarship for need, and she took out a federally guaranteed student loan for $1,700. That comes to $360 more than the bursar goes—and she spent the rest on books, supplies and an occasional movie.

Cyndy would never have been in college were it not for her package of scholarships, job and loan. But the cost of higher education today—it averages $6,100 for private colleges and tops $10,000 at some places—challenges all but the wealthiest families. The Federal government helps millions of students; currently, one out of every three, more than 4 million in all, receives some form of Federal financial assistance. In line with President Reagan's directive to cut the budget, however, Congress is now slashing Federal aid to education. The ongoing debate is confusing, with committees in the House and Senate in open disagreement about how much money to trim from which programs. The final cut may be as high as $1 billion, primarily from Pell Grants, which are Federal scholarships for needy students, and from the Guaranteed Student Loan program (GSL), through which the government backs and subsidizes low-interest loans for any student regardless of income (chart).

The timing of the Congressional action is particularly important because most scholarship and loan plans are made in spring and early summer. "You have families out there that are already struggling," says Jerold Roschwalb of the National Association of State Universities and Land-Grant Colleges. "They're not sure what kind of assistance they're going to get, and with all this uncertainty, people on campuses can't give them any hard advice." Some educators believe they have an obligation to go along with budget reductions. "President Reagan has a mandate to cut government costs and we can't retain our credibility if we suggest that higher education should be exempt," says Boston University president John Silber. At the same time, they worry that hundreds of thousands of students may have to drop out or change their school plans if the Administration's proposals are approved. Colleges would suffer, too. Some are already in trouble because of declining enrollments—and might not survive further losses. After serious lobbying, the colleges do appear to have won a partial victory: most changes in financing will not hit students until the 1982–83 academic year, giving families and institutions a year to adjust.

Eligibility

Ironically, the contemplated reductions would strike hardest at the middle class that the Reagan Administration pledged to help. New formulas and spending limits would knock tens of thousands of families in the $17,000-to-$25,000 income range from the Pell Grant program. And families earning above $25,000 may lose eligibility for guaranteed student loans, unless they can show special need. Richard Bergovoy, who has just completed his first year at Boston University law school, fears that he may have to drop out to earn his tuition unless he can continue to use GSL. Bergovoy's father makes about $30,000 a year, which is above the possible cutoff point, but there are two other children living at home. "My parents voted for Reagan, and they told me not to worry," Richard says. "Now I think

WHERE SCHOOLS GET THEIR MONEY

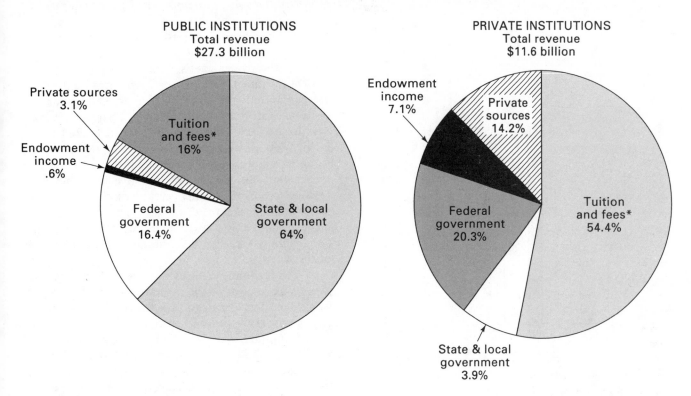

PUBLIC INSTITUTIONS
Total revenue
$27.3 billion

Private sources
3.1%

Endowment
income
.6%

Tuition
and fees*
16%

Federal
government
16.4%

State & local
government
64%

PRIVATE INSTITUTIONS
Total revenue
$11.6 billion

Endowment
income
7.1%

Private
sources
14.2%

Federal
government
20.3%

Tuition
and fees*
54.4%

State & local
government
3.9%

*Includes Federal loans and grants to students

Source: National Education Center for Education Statistics, data for fiscal year 1979

they're learning they were wrong." Even the wife of Presidential counselor Edwin M. Meese III sounds concerned about college costs. "We'll have to take loans to put Scott through Princeton," Ursula Meese recently told a New York Times reporter. "Ed is making $60,000 a year and you don't put a son through school at $11,000 a year on that without taking loans.

The financial adjustments could alter the face of American higher education. As they grew fat with students in the late '60s and early '70s, many institutions enlarged their campuses and their services. When they faced financial stress, they often papered over the gaps with Federal money, brought to them indirectly by the students through loans and grants, "Everybody is nervous about what may happen to the loan program because of the sheer volume of revenue it generates for the higher-education community," says James Moore, a Department of Education financial aid official.

Major reductions will trim the number of low-income students colleges can accept because they don't have sufficient scholarship money. The cuts will divert many students from private to lower-tuition public colleges. "It will be hard to maintain enrollments, particu-

larly in colleges that are not elite," says John Phillips, of the National Association of Independent Colleges and Universities. "Sometimes the student's decision is more of a marketing choice than an educational choice."

Formula

The Federal government provides assistance to college students in several different ways. The GI Bill, for example, is aimed at specific recipients, but most other aid is much less restricted. The two biggest programs are the Pell Grants and Guaranteed Student Loans. Pell Grants (named after Rhode Island Sen. Claiborne Pell) are direct scholarships awarded under a formula that considers the size of a family and its income, assets and expenses. Under the current formula, for instance, a student can qualify for a Pell Grant if he is one of two children and his parents earn less than $25,000 a year. The plan started modestly enough in 1973 with grants to students averaging $269 and Federal costs of about $122 million. In 1978, Congress eased family-income requirements, and in the academic year just ending, an estimated 2.6 million students received

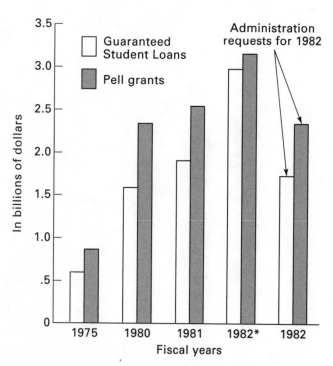

HOW THE GOVERNMENT HELPS

Guaranteed Student Loans

Pell grants

Administration requests for 1982

In billions of dollars

3.5

3.0

2.5

2.0

1.5

1.0

.5

0

1975   1980   1981   1982*   1982

Fiscal years

*Congressional Budget Office estimates

Source: Office of Management and Budget

Pell Grants averaging nearly $1,000—at cost to the government of about $2.4 billion.

Guaranteed Student Loans are an attempt to leverage Federal money in the private sector. Under GSL, the student borrows from a private lender, usually a bank, and the government both guarantees repayment and subsidizes the interest. The program began in 1966 with 6 per cent loans for students from families earning $15,000 or less. It took off after 1978, when Congress eliminated the family-income ceiling so that any student—regardless of his parents' income—could get a GSL. Currently, under-graduates are eligible to borrow as much as $2,500 a year, up to a total of $12,500. The government pays all the interest while they are in school, and everything above 9 per cent afterward. When they leave school, students have ten years to repay the principal plus 9 per cent interest. GSL's will cost the government an estimated $1.9 billion in the current fiscal year.*

---

*Congress last year also authorized a separate 9 per cent guaranteed-loan program for parents of college sudents. So far, banks in only one state, Massachusetts, have made loans under this plan.

Awash in good intentions, Congress neglected to put a firm spending cap on either of these major entitlement programs, and in the past three years they have spiraled almost out of control. One thing Congress did not anticipate was the stunning rise in interest rates. As a result, the government's most recent payments have been at the rate of 18.6 per cent. And because the loans are guaranteed, the government must make good any defaults, which are running about 12 per cent; it manages to get back only about half the defaulted funds. Finally, by eliminating the GSL family-income test, Congress allowed not just the middle class but the rich to benefit. This has made it possible for some savvy families to borrow at 9 per cent, invest the money at 16 per cent and pocket the difference. But since no one can make a killing this way, financial-aid authorities maintain that only a small number of families take advantage of the gimmick.

The recommendations now pending in Congress take an ax to most of the overgrowth. The House plan would limit Pell Grants to $1,800 a year per student, no matter what his demonstrated need—a reduction of $300 from the currently authorized figure. The Senate would cap the Pell program at $2.8 billion, and reduce individual grants if the money ran out. As for GSL's, the House Education and Labor Committee proposed a plan last week that would allow all families to remain eligible. But the committee's plan would require students to pay a 4 per cent fee when they get a loan, thus reducing the costs of the interest subsidies paid by the Federal government. The Senate would put a $25,000-income ceiling on GSL's, except in cases of demonstrated need (several children in college, for instance), and would charge a 5 per cent loan assessment fee. The prognosis for all of these changes, plus cuts in other programs, is still so "murky," says Charles Saunders of the American Council on Education, that "the only thing clear is that it won't be solved until the House-Senate conference."

Collapse

Higher-education lobbyists seem willing to take the hand Congress deals them on the Pell Grants, but they are nursing their chips on GSL's. Their major concern is that the Reagan Administration will try to make students pay their own interest while in school. If that plan succeeds, says Saunders, "the GSL program will collapse because so many banks will pull out." Elimination of the in-school subsidy would require the banks, instead of merely billing the government quarterly, to monitor loans and dun students for interest. "I hope we've convinced the Senate that if they end interest subsidies, they would end GSL," says Robert J. Spiller, president of the Boston Five Cents Savings Bank, which will make $25 million in GSL loans this year. "A bank couldn't take the risk of not collecting from a student or having to defer its interest income for four years."

Most educators argue that big budget cuts that would force large numbers of students to drop out of college are a short-sighted saving. "The government is spending about $2 billion a year [under GSL] to support $20 billion in credit to students," says Paul Borden, president of the Association of Student Loan Funds. "That's an outstanding bargain for the government, the students and the institutions." The question Congress must decide is what kind of investment it wants to make in the country's next generation of human capital. ■

QUESTIONS

1. What do you consider to be the benefits of your higher education?
2. a. What arguments would you provide in favor of government intervention in the market for higher education?
   b. Would there be any "market failure" in the absence of government aid to college students?
3. Consider the government subsidies for higher education mentioned in this article:
   a. Briefly describe the subsidies associated with the GSL (Guaranteed Student Loan) program.
   b. Based on your answer to question 2, do you agree or disagree with the statement by Paul Borden in the last paragraph? (Note: In Selection 52, the article by economist Alan Blinder will provide a more formal framework in which to answer such a question.)
4. Decide whether each of the following arguments justifies government subsidies of the type provided by the GSL program:
   a. Higher education increases the productivity of our labor force.
   b. Fewer students would attend college without the GSL program.
5. Do you think the federal aid policies in existence at the time this article was written (1981) redistribute income from the rich to the poor or vice versa? Explain.
6. Can you think of any reasons why it might make economic sense for the government to guarantee but not subsidize student loans for higher education?

This article deals with arsenic air pollution from a copper smelter in Tacoma, Washington. The article offers numerous details about various attitudes concerning pollution control and the benefits and costs of pollution control. The questions accompanying the article concern the optimal amount of pollution, the benefits and costs of pollution control, and the externality nature of the pollution problem.

What Cost a Life? EPA Asks Tacoma

By ELEANOR RANDOLPH

TACOMA, Wash.—The bankers, the lawyers and the young professionals in expensive cowboy boots talk about this former industrial boomtown as a "New Seattle"—a place where aging smokestacks now coexist with a new convention center and antique stores that sell starched Victorian nightshirts for what was once a day's wages.

Amid the euphoria of their renaissance, however, people in Tacoma are tormented by pressure to take a public position on a grim question, a life-and-death issue that may never have been presented quite so bluntly to any community in the nation.

[A] On the one hand, they can sacrifice the jobs of 570 local residents, banish a $30-million-a-year payroll from a community that has known hard times and weaken the tax base that supports the police, the fire department and other vital services.

Or they can decide to keep all those material benefits—and let one more Tacoma citizen die of lung cancer every year.

Smelter Pours Out Arsenic

At the center of the controversy is a 90-year-old copper smelter, a battered hodgepodge of buildings that the Environmental Protection Agency says is spewing more than 310 tons of arsenic into Tacoma's air every year, spreading the known carcinogen over a circle 12½ miles wide. EPA has designed a plan for cutting the airborne arsenic emissions almost in half, but this half-a-loaf plan still would leave enough arsenic pouring into the air to cause one more lung-cancer death each year than would occur normally.

Yet tougher action to curb the arsenic pollution

probably would force the smelter to close, EPA specialists calculate.

The question for Tacoma is whether it would rather cut the pollution in half, keep the plant open—and suffer one more cancer death each year—or demand further pollution controls and risk losing the smelter's payroll.

Trade-offs between economic benefits and greater health or safety are made all the time in everyday life, of course; automobiles could be made virtually crash-proof, for instance, but they would be prohibitively expensive. But the decisions on such questions usually are made indirectly—implicitly instead of explicitly.

Confrontation Deliberate

What sets the Tacoma situation apart is that the federal government has called upon the people most immediately affected to state explicitly and publicly how safe they want to be. William D. Ruckelshaus, the new administrator of the Environmental Protection Agency, deliberately created the confrontation as a way of focusing national attention on the interplay between costs and benefits that is involved in cleaning up the environment.

And he is not surprised that many in Tacoma are confused, even angry at being asked to state a preference.

"Listen, I know people don't like these kinds of decisions," Ruckelshaus said in an interview with The Times. "Welcome to the world of regulation. People have demanded to be involved and now I have involved them and they say: 'Don't ask that question.'

"What's the alternative? Don't involve them? Then you're accused of doing something nefarious.

"My view is that these are the kinds of tough, balancing questions that we're involved in here in this country in trying to regulate all kinds of hazardous substances. I don't like these questions either, but the societal issue is what risks are we willing to take and for what benefits?''

Taking the Community's Pulse

Legally, Ruckelshaus himself must make the final decision by early next year on how much abatement to demand from Tacoma's smelter, which is run by ASARCO Inc., a major national smelting firm. But he is presenting the issue directly to the community through four workshops in the weeks ahead, followed by a hearing scheduled Nov. 2.

Beside the difficulties of explaining this issue, EPA officials are faced with an even tougher task of taking the community's pulse. Do you poll the community, counting on a random sample? Do you count the pros and cons at the massive hearing that could run to two days or more? One EPA official has suggested a postcard vote.

"We just don't know yet how we are going to do this," said Robert Jacobson, EPA press spokesman in Seattle.

Already, the debate has stirred strong feelings. Some critics of Ruckelshaus' approach challenge EPA's analysis and statistics. Others recoil at the thought of putting a price on a neighbor's job, or worse, a friend's life. Still others bridle at being asked to consider such a difficult, anguishing philosophical question at all; that's the government's job, they say.

No Consensus

And on the central question, there so far is no consensus on what to do about the airborne arsenic, which spreads in a circle that extends from a scorched, desert-like area near the smelter's smokestack to the lush forests of Vashon and Maury islands across the bay, overland to golf courses dampened to a blue-green by the eternal rainful, and, ironically, even over a new, multi-million-dollar downtown development financed by a subsidiary of Ruckelshaus' old employer, Weyerhaeuser Inc.

[B] "Some of us don't understand why EPA is doing this," said Linda Tanz, who is active on environmental issues for the Tacoma League of Women Voters. "EPA came in recently and found that our drinking water was contaminated and just cleaned it up, saying they'd find out why later. Now, why aren't they just cleaning this mess up instead of asking people how much cancer they would like to have? It's a very confusing, difficult issue."

Charlie Davis, a 49-year-old contractor from the small community of Fife, downwind from the smelter, said he and his wife are tired of not raising vegetables because of the arsenic fallout and they are unhappy about the metallic taste in their mouths some days when the wind shifts in their direction.

But Davis has a hard time understanding why his community is deciding something that engineers and government officials are appointed and elected to decide. "They're the experts, aren't they? We don't want extra cancer, but I also hate to see those people lose their jobs. It looks to me like they should be able to catch some of that arsenic and use it."

Some Doubt Hazard

Some Tacomans simply deny that arsenic poses any hazard at all. "I don't feel there's an arsenic problem. It's all mass hysteria," said Loretta Prettyman, the town clerk in Ruston, the half-mile square community where the ASARCO smelter provides the most jobs and a hefty tax base.

"Arsenic doesn't cause cancer. Nothing about it causes cancer. We've had so much flak over the years about the big, bad smelter that we just turn it off."

The balancing of risks and benefits is a controversial political issue when it involves health matters, but experts in the fledgling field of "risk assessment" say that some Americans are beginning to understand that there is no such thing as a risk-free world. In a recent discussion of the subject, the Journal of the American Medical Assn. noted that people voluntarily assume risks all the time—ranging from the risk of smoking 20 cigarettes a day, which causes one death per 200 smokers a year, to the risk of driving a car, which brings one death per 5,900 drivers a year, to the risk of riding motorcycles, a much more dangerous activity that causes one death per 50 riders a year.

But the same people feel differently about community risks, especially risks that can be fixed—such as hazardous wastes that can be removed with enough money and time or a bridge that should be shored up with community taxes.

Accountability an Issue

As Walter R. Lynn, director of the Program on Science, Technology and Society at Cornell University, said, "People don't mind being accountable for the safety of decisions that they make themselves, but they may want absolute safety in situations where they feel that someone else is imposing a risk on them that they don't want to bear."

"In the past, politicians and some judges have said that human life is beyond all price and that sounds fine," said William H. Lowrance, author of a 1976 book on the subject called "Of Acceptable Risk."

"Vaccines and auto safety devices, medical procedures and airplane landing systems do have a price. It's not that we're paying for life—you could make autos with incredibly low risks that cost $100,000 each," Lowrance said. "In the end, we compare protection measures. We argue whether it's worth putting more money into an airport for even lower risks or whether to spend that same money on a new vaccine or reduction of acid rain."

Lowrance argued at the Royal College of Physicians in London last spring that science has now progressed to the point that often "we know enough to 'worry' but not enough to know how much to worry. . . . Scientific knowledge has progressed enormously and we even have the luxury of going around searching for possible trouble."

Such a "luxury" can be compared with tougher times, at the turn of the century, when most farmers used a compound called "Paris green" a harsh, poisonous chemical that killed animals and sometimes people along with agricultural pests.

In Tacoma, specifically, the smelter as it is now operating—without any new equipment to cut down arsenic emissions—is causing about four more lung cancer deaths each year than would be normal in a population of the area's size, according to EPA statisticians. What is proposed is the installation of massive hoods to reduce the amount of arsenic escaping from the smelters' two huge vats of molten metal. If the $4.5-million hoods are installed, EPA estimates, an average of one additional person over the normal annual death rate still would die from lung cancer in this area. Seventy-one to 94 people died here annually in the 1970s from the disease. The risk of lung-cancer death in Tacoma is 20% higher than the national rate.

By shifting much of the psychological burden to the community for what is legally his own decision under the Clean Air Act, Ruckelshaus is acknowledging that scientists do not have the final answers on many environmental questions.

There is almost always an argument, even about the science of an issue. For one thing, there is the "threshold" question. That is, with any particular toxic chemical or substance, is there an exposure level below which *no* damage will be done? Or is the substance so toxic—and the factors determining how individuals react so complex—that *any* level of exposure, no matter how small, always will produce some damage.

Is There a Threshold?

In the Tacoma case, EPA, the National Cancer Institute and other health organizations say there is no threshold for arsenic; even the smallest amounts of arsenic in the air would cause cancers if exposed to enough different kinds of people—all of them reacting in different ways over the years to the poison, scientists at these organizations say.

Lawrence W. Lindquist, manager of the ASARCO plant, takes the other side of this almost-classic environmental argument. He says there is a threshold—an exposure point below which arsenic no longer

causes health problems. He argues that "toxicity depends on concentration"—a lot of arsenic, like a lot of alcohol, is dangerous. A little bit may not hurt, may even be beneficial.

"It's hard for us to understand how we can make an informed decision and inform the people when they've got so many bad numbers," Lindquist said as he was interviewed in his stark offices near the gates of the smelting plant. "We have yet to see any scientific evidence that arsenic causes cancer. We don't see a risk-benefit problem (because) we see no discernible risk here."

EPA Study Called 'Baloney'

Dr. Samuel Milham Jr., head of the epidemiology section of the Washington State Department of Social and Health Services, said that arsenic is indeed carcinogenic, but he contends the EPA projections of possible lung cancers in the area are "baloney."

"I don't believe any of it," said Milham, who added that he has done a "ton of studies" on the Tacoma community and has found no evidence of any increase in lung cancers because of the smelter.

[C] Milham said that studies very clearly show that workers can get cancer from exposure to high levels of arsenic on the job and a study of ASARCO retirees showed that eight times as many died of lung cancer as the normal rate for such deaths in any community.

"But we have been looking for extra lung cancers in the community (among those who do not work at the smelter) and we haven't found them. Nothing," he said.

After the residents of the Tacoma area near Milham at the Nov. 2 hearing, they will then hear the other side from Dana Davoli, an environmental scientist with EPA in Seattle.

"We haven't shown which people are dying in the community, but that doesn't mean they aren't," Davoli said. "This is a projection based on the best health information we know; we can't wait for dead bodies. If we could document the increase in lung cancers, it would already be too late. It would be an epidemic."

The bankers and businessmen in the community—who kicked off a $1.6-million "New Beginnings" ad campaign to bring new business to Tacoma the day Ruckelshaus announced the cancer-versus-jobs dilemma—are hoping that the increasingly strident debate in their city will not be bad for business.

James K. Anderson, president of Pacific First Federal Savings Bank, said that he and other businessmen worry that "it will become an emotional issue so that all the true issues here don't get aired."

He added that even though publicity about the smelter may have hurt the "New Beginnings" project by making some businessmen wary of bringing their families to Tacoma, a quick, emotional decision that results in the closing of ASARCO could also hurt the "business climate" of the community.

"It's a two-edged sword. There's also a lot of concern whether this community would treat a member of the business establishment fairly," Anderson said.

Motives Questioned

Brian Baird, president of Tacomans for a Healthy Environment, worries that it is all an effort by Ruckelshaus and his former business associates to get the environmentalists to take the blame for clearing the way for newer, cleaner industries so people will no longer joke, as they have in the past, about "the aroma of Tacoma."

"It would be real nice for those guys if the environmentalists get out the smelter and they take the heat for cleaning up Tacoma's image," Baird said.

However, Ruckelshaus said that the choice of Tacoma as the first big battleground on risk analysis was "coincidental." He added that even though he was an executive vice president for Weyerhaeuser before coming to EPA, he has not heard from Weyerhaeuser officials on the issue. He called such contacts "the kind of input I don't need from the community." And in spite of the fact that a subsidiary of Weyerhaeuser, Community Development Corp., is spending $100 million to redevelop parts of the Tacoma downtown, Ruckelshaus sees no reason why he cannot make the final decision on the smelter question.

"I have no sense at all that I am not completely objective about this decision," he said.

Indeed, even complete objectivity may not be enough for a community that is becoming increasingly involved in the question. The Bellevue Washington Journal demanded in an editorial: "Who speaks for the guy with lung cancer? Who will teach his children to fish or buy funeral bouquets in gratitude for his sacrifice on behalf of 'all of us here in the smelter'?"

As the argument in the community becomes more complex and people begin to understand what is being weighed in the balance, many feel more and more strongly that the decision should not be theirs. It belongs to the experts, but to experts people can trust.

"The most natural first reaction from people would be—why do I have to decide?" said Lester B. Lave, professor of economics and public policy at Carnegie Mellon University in Pittsburgh. "Until fairly recently, we had this impulse as a society to trust such matters to the experts. We would believe them, by and large—the experts on nuclear power, chemical industry, who told us things were safe. But in this last generation, experts say it is safe and we say 'I don't believe you.'"

"In the end, we may have to come back to trust the experts, because for most people these hard choices are too painful. If somebody close by got lung cancer, we would wonder if we caused it. Nobody likes to have on their conscience that they allowed two or three more lung-cancer deaths in their community."

As Lave puts it: "Ultimately, if we don't trust the experts, then we have to make the decision. That's what is happening here." ∎

QUESTIONS

1. Consider passage B:
   a. How would you respond to Linda Tanz's question?
   b. How much pollution should we tolerate? Explain briefly.
2. In a diagram with the quantity of arsenic pollution on the horizontal axis, depict both the marginal cost of the pollution damage to Tacoma's residents and the copper smelter's marginal cost of reducing pollution (or, equivalently, the smelter's marginal benefit from being allowed to pollute). Assume that the pollution costs are an externality from the perspective of the copper smelter. Use your diagram to indicate
   a. The initial level of Tacoma's arsenic air pollution
   b. The level of pollution if the smelter is shut down
   c. The efficient level of pollution
3. Based on evidence from the article, if Tacoma's arsenic air pollution is reduced:
   a. What types of benefits will result?
   b. What types of costs might result?
4. Select the best answer to the following question and briefly support your choice: In passage A, the "$30 million-a-year" cost (due to lost jobs and payroll) of a shutdown of Tacoma's copper smelter
   a. Overstates the true economic cost of the shutdown
   b. Understates the true economic cost of the shutdown
   c. Correctly states the true economic cost of the shutdown
5. Consider passage C: If Dr. Milham is correct, then is it possible to argue that the health risk is not an externality problem? Why or why not?

This article on highway congestion illustrates how common externalities actually are. The article deals with the issues of peak versus off-peak highway use and details some recent innovations in the metering of traffic. The questions include a quantitative problem on the external costs of congestion and cover additional issues, such as the nature of congestion, other places where it occurs, and metering innovations discussed in the article.

How to Break Up Traffic Jams

By JONATHAN MARSHALL

From San Francisco to Houston to New York City, ordinary citizens worry less about the threat of nuclear war or the Latin debt crisis than whether they will emerge each day of sound mind and body from nightmarish traffic jams.

In the luckiest cities, billions of dollars invested in new highways, heavy rail systems and subsidized buses have bought only a few years' relief from inevitable gridlock. Elsewhere, policies of simply increasing the supply of transportation have proved to be wildly expensive failures.

Urban Americans can't afford to ignore the demand side of the equation any longer. No strategy to solve traffic woes will work unless individual drivers pay the full costs they impose on society. The answer isn't a punitive crackdown on private autos, but rather a fair and equitable levy on their use of the roads.

Politicians and transit planners have ducked the issue of road pricing as unrealistic and unworkable. But engineering solutions today make the economists' case for road pricing unanswerable. And government officials may change their tune. Last week, New York City's transportation commissioner, Ross Sandler, said that "dramatic" steps were needed to curb city traffic congestion. Among the possible proposals he mentioned: charging motorists fees for entering certain areas.

Randall Pozdena, a transportation specialist at the Federal Reserve Bank of San Francisco, observes that highway-user charges are "perhaps the most important issue in transportation policy. Transportation impacts land use, commerce, energy and the environment in very direct and important ways. To make sensible policy in these other areas, we must know what the highway system costs us and what the effects of changing our policy might be. Brute force policies in these other areas may be much less successful and more costly than a rational highway pricing mechanism.''

The Law of Peak-Hour Congestion

Giving cars a free ride on highways is like giving desert dwellers free water for lawns, pools and golf courses: They'll use everything you give them. The Law of Peak-Hour Congestion follows: Traffic always grows to fill the available capacity.

Rush-hour auto commuters pay for only a fraction of what they take from society in terms of clean air, police services, road grants from the general fund and, most of all, lost time from traffic.

[A] A single driver's decision to enter a bottleneck may cost him only a few extra minutes of expensive commuting time. Totaled over thousands of drivers, congestion costs amount to millions of dollars every year on major arteries.

Also significant are subsidies to meet the physical demands of rush-hour drivers. Typically, less than a third of highway traffic occurs at or near peak times in the major direction. Yet this minority of drivers dictates the size of the road. In the Los Angeles basin, according to one academic estimate from the mid-1970s, this subsidy totals at least $250 a year for every rush-hour commuter. (Prices have about doubled since then.)

[B] University of California economists estimated 10 years ago that if Bay Area roads were priced to reflect the full costs of traffic, rush-hour charges in the central city would reach 28 cents a mile and eight cents in less dense urban zones.

Off-peak charges might amount to only a penny a mile. Yet the California gas tax today comes to only six-tenths of a cent per mile. Most transportation maladies can be traced directly to this handsome subsidy. Since individual autos pay so little at rush hour, people move farther from work in search of cheap land, causing sprawl, pollution, wasted energy—and more traffic jams. Faced with more traffic, long-distance commuters demand more highways, further burdening the public treasury. Transit agencies, public or private, too often wither in the face of such heavily subsidized competition.

Proper road pricing could work a dramatic cure. Faced with paying their fair share at rush hour, many more commuters would stagger their work hours and take carpools or mass transit, unjamming the roads. All vehicles would run faster as a result, netting most commuters a substantial cost saving in time beyond their road fees. With faster turnaround times, bus systems would make more efficient use of vehicles and drivers, and would appeal to many more riders. Air pollution would drop immediately. And, last but not least, the public could save a fortune by postponing or canceling new highway construction and by cutting back subsidies to competing transit operations.

With proper planning and explanation, there's every reason to think the public would welcome a pricing test. After all, people already pay for the roads; the proceeds of a road-use fee would replace existing taxes and finance new construction where warranted, not disappear into a black hole. Unlike general taxes, such fees would fall more fairly on drivers in proportion to their burden on society.

Just as people expect to pay for such basic services as water and electricity, they should quickly adapt to rush-hour road fees. All the more so since consumers don't seem to mind paying differential rates depending on the time (hour, day or season) for movies, air flights, telephone calls, fruits and vegetables and even some public transit. People understand that when supplies of a good are limited and demand is high, prices go up. Peak-hour road space is no different.

All very fine in theory, but how would road pricing work in practice? No one wants to fumble for change and stop every mile at a toll booth. Fortunately, better alternatives have already been proven in numerous applications at home and abroad.

In 1975, Singapore introduced a simple auto-license sticker to charge low-occupancy cars entering the crowded city center at peak morning hours. At $1.40 a day or $30 a month, it immediately cut congestion 40%. A small force of traffic police located at entry points keeps drivers honest at low cost to the city.

Hong Kong undertook a more elaborate Electronic Road Pricing experiment from 1983 to 1985. Cars equipped with a small, solid-state electronic license plate automatically identified themselves to sensing loops in the road connected to a central computer. The computer recorded the tolls and billed car owners each month. The system permitted total flexibility as to which roads to toll and what to charge.

The experiment showed the technology to be "quite simple and of proven reliability," in the words of one government report. Politically it failed, however; motorists came away unconvinced that their fees would be offset by lower taxes. Some also objected to having their routes monitored by computer, despite the greater intrusiveness of bank and telephone records. (Anyone wanting to give the government the slip could just take a taxi.)

Similar technologies are already in use in the U.S. In 1984 the state of Oregon installed electronic transponders at several weigh stations to speed up truck identification and clearance. Participating trucks with electronic license plates can roll over weigh-in-motion scales without ever stopping. Everyone saves time and gains information. "It's a great management tool for government, a great fleet management tool and especially useful for monitoring trucks carrying hazardous materials," notes Barbara Koos, an analyst with the Oregon Department of Transportation. The encouraging results have prompted 13 states to expand the experiment and develop standards. Beginning next year, the so-called Crescent Project will establish common electronic truck identification systems from the Washington–British Columbia border to Texas.

The New York–New Jersey Port Authority plans to affix electronic license plates that will assess tolls on about 3,000 buses passing daily through the Lincoln Tunnel. Faster and less grumpy than human toll collectors, the system "should help provide an accurate reading of vehicles, speed traffic and minimize pollution and time constraints," says Joe Klementowicz, a senior engineer on the project. "If it works, we'll be looking at other vehicle populations. There is the possibility of going to private autos."

Absence of Political Will

Electronic identifiers already serve cars in some private parking lots. And California's state transportation agency (Caltrans) is testing an electronic car ID system at the Coronado Bridge in San Diego. "My hope would be that we could use them on all nine toll bridges we operate," says Caltrans's project director Jerry Meis. "The big plus for Caltrans is fewer collectors and for motorists it's convenience."

Electronic systems should cost drivers less than $20 a "tag." These small, rugged devices are powered by a transmitter at the tolling point and should last the lifetime of the car.

Some transit authorities prefer lower-tech optical scanners of the sort used at supermarket checkout stands (only much more reliable). Drivers purchase bar-coded stickers for their rear windows—or their helmets in the case of motorcyclists. In use by the Delaware River Port Authority for 15 years, the system's reliability exceeds 99%, according to Stan Shultz, vice president of Automatic Toll Systems in Mount Vernon, N.Y.

The technology is cheap, too. For only $20 a day, toll authorities can save at least four human collectors per lane. The stickers themselves cost only about 65 cents each to produce and are nearly impossible to counterfeit.

Take your pick: The technology is here to do the job. All that stands in the way of relieving traffic misery is an absence of political will. Commuters of the world unite, you have nothing to lose but endless delays on the road. ■

QUESTIONS

1. Suppose that during rush hour in California's Bay Area, each additional car on the road adds an average of five seconds to the commuting time of two hundred other people. Suppose also that people value their time at $9 per hour (¼ cent per second).
   a. What is the total dollar value of the costs that each additional driver imposes on other drivers?
   b. With no congestion tolls, will there be too few, too many, or just the right number of Bay Area drivers during rush hour? Explain briefly.
   c. If congestion tolls could easily be charged, how much should each driver pay during rush hour in order to have the efficient number of cars on the road?

2. Consider passage A: Is this "cost" an externality to the driver? If so, why? If not, then what, if any, externality is associated with rush-hour commuting?
3. Consider passage B: Why should traffic charges vary so much over time?
4. Several years ago it may have been reasonable to simply put up with peak-period congestion, but judging from the article, today we should do something about it. What innovations make it more feasible now than in the past to charge drivers for peak-period highway use?
5. Name two or three other economic activities that are subject to periodic congestion.

This article illustrates both how common and how problematic public goods are. The article reports on the rising amount of theft of "intellectual property" such as cable TV signals and computer software. The questions concern the particular market failure that plagues the private production of these goods, and the efficiency issues that are at stake.

Can Software Be Made Safe from Piracy?

By RALPH VARTABEDIAN

[A] Each evening in homes across Southern California, mom, dad and the kids warm up their favorite couch and switch on an illegal television receiver to steal the broadcast signals of California Subscription Television Service.

This seemingly innocuous act of tuning in the television station without paying a fee has become a popular form of electronic-era bravado among many otherwise law-abiding households, even though it violates no fewer than a half dozen federal and state statutes, according to the pay-TV firm. The company estimates that 50,000 homes steal its signal in this fashion.

Such theft of electronic data is growing in popularity on a broad scale, part of what some industry officials see as a high-technology crime wave that is permeating some of the healthiest and fastest-growing segments of the U.S. economy.

Breakdown in Protection

[B] The greatly heralded age of information and technology is finally arriving in offices and homes across the nation. But as illustrated by the growing popularity—and widespread public acceptance—of stealing pay-TV signals, there has been a breakdown along the way in the locks and doors that historically have protected all kinds of so-called "intellectual property."

At issue is how to preserve creators' rights to valuable new information and ideas in a society that has thrived for centuries on a free intellectual marketplace.

"As we enter the information age with all the aspects of automating the treatment of information, we have essentially produced information as an intangible asset subject to crime," say Donn Parker, one of the nation's top computer-crime experts and a consultant at SRI International, a research firm in Menlo Park, Calif.

Meanwhile, there is mounting litigation between corporations based on a hodgepodge of unclear case law that governs the rapidly changing area of intellectual property rights.

The problems are multiplying partly because ever greater amounts of society's wealth no longer are physical assets that can be locked up. New ideas, manufacturing processes, data bases and basic technology represent some of the most important forms of wealth today.

"Intellectual assets are unlike financial assets or physical assets," says Henry Hanson, director of intellectual property at Minneapolis-based Honeywell Inc. "It is a little bit like catching smoke in your hand sometimes. They are dynamic. They are intangible."

What qualifies today as intellectual property is indeed far-flung: Everything from the innards of Pac-Man to the huge data banks of personal information kept on virtually every American by government agencies, credit bureaus and others. Intellectual property also describes such things as the satellite transmissions of sporting events and the industrial technology used to manufacture computer chips.

One measure of how the growth of intellectual property has exploded is the volume of copyrighted material nationwide. In just the past decade, the annual volume of new copyright filings has jumped 40%, according to the Library of Congress.

Governments as well as the owners of this new property are struggling to find ways to integrate it properly into established legal and commercial structures.

Tax experts, for example, are examining how some taxes might be applied to intellectual property in the same manner that they apply to physical property, according to Gary Jugum, assistant chief counsel for the California Board of Equalization.

For instance, California sales tax applies to software sold on a computer disk. But if the software is sold and transferred electronically, there is no tax—an obvious contradiction in tax theory since the product is the same.

These issues are so new that authority for dealing with them is widely dispersed throughout agencies of government, law enforcement and the courts. Corporations are just beginning to take a unified approach to intellectual property management.

Short-Term Solution

On a practical level the problems sometimes seem insurmountable. California Subscription Television, for example, figures it would have to spend $2 million on new scrambling devices to shut off the estimated 50,000 pirates of its signal. But the firm has been reluctant to spend that kind of money because it believes it will only give manufacturers of illegal devices one more product to market.

"These people are really business parasites," says Mark Edelman, until recently a vice president at the firm. "We go through the burden of setting up the business and paying all the copyright fees. All they do is develop a device to steal all that."

Determining exactly how widespread such violations are is difficult because so far nobody has kept statistics on reported offenses.

[C] **Nevertheless, a high-tech underground seems to be flourishing. Take, for example, the proliferation across Southern California of electronic bulletin boards set up by personal-computer users for the illegal trading of computer programs. To get access to the bulletin boards requires a home computer and a telephone. The caller hooks his computer into another computer that advertises various pirated software packages for sale. An entire transaction can be handled over the telephone between two strangers.**

"You don't even have to look someone in the eye when you pirate a computer program," observes Parker, of SRI. "In the computer software field, I have had computer company executives tell me that for every copy of their programs that they sell, two of them are pirated. I don't know if that is typical, but that's why we are beginning to study it," Parker adds.

Violations Are Rampant

Such computer software piracy has been outlawed since the early 1970s, when copyright privileges were extended to software. Nevertheless, violations are rampant, and many experts are clearly concerned about the potential consequences.

"Copyright is very directly related to a free society," says Mel Ninner, a copyright specialist at the UCLA law school. "If we are going to have an open society and artistic, literary and scholarly creativity that is not (government) controlled, then we have got to rely on the creators earning their living from the marketplace."

"It takes a long time for the legal system to react, and, in the meantime, you have an enormous industry that is expanding rapidly and moving into new areas," says James Pooley, a Silicon Valley attorney specializing in trade secret law.

California, Massachusetts, Minnesota and Florida are at the forefront in examining these new issues, but getting new laws passed even in those states has proven a major hurdle.

All too frequently, existing laws must be bent to fit high-technology crimes, some experts say. For example, when two Philadelphia programmers were arrested for stealing $144,000 worth of computer time several years ago, they were formally charged with mail fraud because there were no appropriate statutes, Parker says.

At the same time, corporations are ending up in court more often because civil laws are unclear about intellectual property rights.

By any measure, electronics and computer manufacturers have the biggest problem protecting their technology and developing safeguards.

So far, no computer system has ever been built with electronic security measures that cannot be penetrated by unauthorized users. So-called military "tiger teams" have demonstrated that even the Pentagon's own Worldwide Military Command and Control System computer is not tamper-proof, according to Pentagon sources.

It is difficult to prevent disaffected or avaricious employees from peddling a company's critical secret knowledge to buyers on the outside, industry officials say.

"We could totally bar the doors and pull the shades on all of the windows, strip search employees as they go out and X-ray them to make sure they didn't swallow something," says Honeywell's Hanson. "You could just carry it to an extreme that would just be totally unacceptable." ∎

QUESTIONS

1. Do passages A and C deal with public goods or private goods? Briefly explain your decision.
2. Would your answer to question 1 change if the goods could be more effectively protected? Why or why not?
3. With no government intervention in markets for "intellectual property," what, if any, market failure would tend to result?

4. Consider passage B: Indicate how, if at all, each of the following might enhance economic efficiency (consider each one separately):
   a. Preserving "creators' rights"
   b. "Stealing pay-TV signals"

In this article economist Alan Blinder provides a clear statement of the two criteria of efficiency and equity. He also suggests the following "apolitical litmus test" for evaluating public policy changes:

> Hard-headed *and* soft-hearted policies, i.e., those that improve effi-
> ciency *and* redistribute income from rich to poor, should be adopted.
> Soft-headed *and* hard-hearted policies, i.e., those that reduce efficiency
> *and* redistribute income from the poor to the rich, should be avoided.

When there is a trade-off between efficiency and equity,
Blinder simply says that reasonable people have the right to
disagree. Blinder's "test" can be applied to many of the policy
questions raised throughout the articles in this book.

Economic Policy Can Be
Hard-Headed—and Soft-Hearted

By ALAN S. BLINDER

Five years ago, widespread dissatisfaction with economic policy helped Ronald Reagan sweep Jimmy
Carter out of office. Candidate Reagan apparently
struck a responsive chord with the voters when he argued that Democratic policies had been too much concerned with redistribution and too little concerned with
preserving the incentives necessary to make the free-
market system work. The Democrats, in a word, had
been soft-hearted but soft-headed.

The Reagan revolution, at least in its rhetoric,
promised to change all that. National economic policy
was to become more hard-headed about market incentives and more hard-hearted toward the poor. To un-
leash the energies of the private sector, marginal tax
rates on the rich had to come down. The poor would
have to learn the virtue of self-reliance.

The Reagan policy initiatives were popular at first.
Still, some party poopers did worry that large deficits
would push up real interest rates, harming investment
and growth. Others fretted that the corporate tax breaks
would unduly distort the pattern of investment by imposing radically different tax rates on different types of
investments. A few bleeding hearts wondered out loud

how the poor and near-poor would muddle through. All
of these worries proved well-founded.

I want to argue here that we can do better than
either the hard-headed, hard-hearted policies that President Reagan ushered in or the soft-hearted, soft-headed
policies that he chased out. With a little clear thinking—
and a lot less ideological incantation—we can design an
economic policy that is at once soft-hearted and hard-
headed.

Political Whimsy

Such a policy would be founded on two basic principles. The first is that more goods are better than less.
The second is that poorer people are needier than richer
ones. Neither idea strikes me as particularly controversial nor ideological. But much follows from them.

If more is better than less, then we should take
care that our economic policies make our economic system more, not less, productive. Call this the Principle
of Efficiency. For more than two centuries, economists
have stressed that free markets are extraordinarily good
at providing consumers with what they want at the
lowest possible prices. But for much longer, politicians
around the globe have been interfering, sometimes
whimsically, with the operations of free markets. If we
are to make the most of our limited resources, as the
Principle of Efficiency demands, then the burden of
proof ought to fall on those who would interfere with
the market.

Reprinted from August 12, 1985 issue of *Business Week*
by special permission, copyright © 1985 by McGraw-
Hill, Inc.

If the poor have a greater urgency for income than the rich, it follows that a dollar taken from a deep pocket and put in an empty one helps the recipient more than it hurts the (involuntary) donor. Call this the Principle of Equity. This principle provides the intellectual underpinning for redistributive policies, for it implies that assisting society's underdogs is a proper function of government.

Right and Wrong

Historically, the soft-hearted Democratic party has more steadfastly supported the Principle of Equity while the hard-headed Republican party has more vigorously promoted the Principle of Efficiency. But it is not my purpose here to defend one position or party against the other. My point is that both parties have been right—and wrong. A more balanced view recognizes the legitimacy of both Democratic equity and Republican efficiency in a democratic republic such as ours. We need to marry the hard-headed accountant to the soft-hearted social worker. But how?

I suggest the following apolitical litmus test. When a change in economic policy is proposed, we should first ask: Does this policy improve the efficiency of the market system, that is, does it give us more rather than less? If the answer is "no," we should then ask: Does the policy redistribute income from the rich to the Poor? If

the answer is again "no," the proposed policy probably should be rejected. Many poorly conceived economic policies would be avoided by the application of this simple test. Most protectionist measures, for example, redistribute income from the average consumer to wealthy capitalists and to workers whose wages are well above average, and they damage efficiency in the bargain.

If the answers to both of these questions are "yes," then the proposed policy promotes both efficiency and equity and therefore probably merits adoption. For example, by closing tax loopholes, comprehensive tax reform would allow us to lower marginal tax rates, thus improving economic incentives, and to raise the personal exemption, shielding the poor from taxation.

Of course, not all policy proposals are so easily evaluated. Some, like the personal tax cuts of 1981–84, will further the Principle of Efficiency by compromising the Principle of Equity. Others will promote equity by sacrificing efficiency. In these difficult cases, reasonable people may disagree.

But just because the Principles of Equity and Efficiency do not tell us everything does not mean that they do not tell us anything. They do give us some answers. And that is a start in the right direction. ∎

QUESTIONS

1. What is the "Principle of Efficiency"?
2. What is the "Principle of Equity"?
3. According to Blinder, what type of policy changes should clearly be rejected? What type should clearly be adopted? Provide an example of each type.
4. Many policies and policy changes have been raised in the articles in this book. Carefully evaluate the efficiency *and* equity effects of each of the following policies (or policy changes). (The title of the article where the policy is discussed in this book is in parentheses.)
   a. Federal financial aid to college students ("The Cuts in Federal Aid")
   b. Higher minimum wage laws ("The Real Costs of a Higher Minimum Wage")
   c. Rent control laws ("Santa Monica—Only the Elite Need Apply")

   d. Regulation of taxicabs ("The Drive Is on to Deregulate Taxicabs")
   e. Regulation of billboards ("Braude's Ban on New Billboards")
   f. Raising the price of local phone calls from public phones ("Why Calls Should Cost a Quarter")

5. a. Based on your answers to question 4, which of the above policies are "hard-headed and soft-hearted" and therefore, according to Blinder, should be adopted?
   b. Which are "soft-headed and hard-hearted" and therefore, according to Blinder should be dropped?
   c. Which policies, according to Blinder, would be suitable for further debate? Explain briefly.